THE wildlife TRUSTS

SPRING

An anthology for the changing seasons

Edited by Melissa Harrison

&

First published 2016 by
Elliott and Thompson Limited
27 John Street, London WC1N 2BX
www.eandtbooks.com

ISBN: 978-1-78396-223-5

9 8 7 6 5 4 3 2 1

A catalogue record for this book is available from the British Library.

Printed in the UK by TJ International Ltd.

CONTENTS

INTRODUCTION

It is a moment of quickening, of rebirth. The old, lovely story: life surging back, despite everything, once again. However spring finds you – birdsong, blossom or spawn – it is a signal: the earth turning its ancient face back to the sun.

For me it's snowdrops, fat black buds on the ash trees and the blackbird's first song that tell me spring's arrived. I live in a city, as more and more of us do these days, and so the signs seem even more precious, even easier to miss. Each year I seek them out, anxiously, ardently: each year I feel the same atavistic joy as the green world starts to grow and the birds breed.

On these temperate isles we have been bound to the seasons since time immemorial, dependent on the circling year and its ancient pattern of growth and senescence. That our homes are warm and bright all year round, that we can eat what we want whenever we like, are recent developments in evolutionary terms: no surprise, then, that we have not lost, in a few generations, our deep connection to the changing year. Spring's quickening still quickens us, whether villager or urbanite, farmer or commuter. It's in our bones.

And the seasons roll through our literature, too, budding, blossoming, fruiting and dying back. Think of it: the lazy summer days and golden harvests, the misty autumn walks and frozen fields in winter, and all the hopeful romance of spring. Sometimes, as with Chaucer's 'Aprill shoures', the seasons are a way to set the scene; sometimes they are the subject-matter itself – but there's magic in the way a three hundred-year-old account of birdsong, say, can collapse time utterly, granting us a moment of real communion with the past.

Although that sense of changelessness is now, sadly, an illusion. Our busyness, our industry, have altered the world's climate, shifting the timing of many natural phenomena and interfering in natural events that have been happening for millennia. We are also witnessing a widespread, sudden decline in wildlife on these islands, which is changing our experience of all four seasons. And so it is more and more important today that we engage with nature physically, intellectually and emotionally, rather than allow ourselves to disconnect; that we witness rather than turn away, and celebrate rather than neglect.

This book, the first in a new series from The Wildlife Trusts, is an attempt to do just that. A collection of writing both classic and modern, and from all corners of the country, it mixes prose and poetry dating back a thousand years to tell the story of spring's yearly progress across these islands, and remind us of all we have not yet lost. Most excitingly, I think, these four books feature new writing by members of the general public as well as by established authors, adding up to a fittingly diverse range of voices that sing out the season's joy.

'Nothing is so beautiful as Spring', wrote Gerard Manley Hopkins in 1877. He was right.

Melissa Harrison, Spring 2016

In the Northwest Highlands of Scotland, wildlife and landscape are as defined by light and wind as by geology, vegetation and people, and by the yearning for brighter days as the long winter months pass.

Here, on a small croft by the sea, winters are deep and dark, stormy, cold and fierce. There is no easy way out of winter. Its cold, hard grip is periodically loosened when strong, warm, westerly winds blow in from the Atlantic and then our mountains, snow-clad and proud, lose their glistening blankets. Snowmelt waters unite with the tepid storm rains and churn down towards the sea, noisily lighting up the frothing burns and flooding lochans. Fierce squalls batter and pound, whipping up bird, beast, tree, leaf and sea, while rushing snatches of cloud, shower, rainbow and sunbeam paint our hills and croft fields in kaleidoscopic colours. When the winds pause again, hazy, moisture-laden airs diffuse sunlight through pale-lemon and grey veils, and smoothe waves into quicksilver and opal slickness. In these brief remissions of citrine lull and cobweb-light breezes, a sense of expectation grows, along with a discernible shifting of the light and subtle extension of the days. Winter is ending.

As the sun sinks low each late-winter day, the ground, bleached pale, reflects the dying light and for a few short breaths turns pink and purple, as though the earth itself knows that spring is coming. Growing midday brightness is flanked by this surreptitious, dwindling luminosity, when hill, sky and sea merge in opaque diffuseness. Making the most of these tranquil interludes, birds call out, chattering and gossiping, organising each other and arranging feathers in accordance with the latest fashions. Along the shore, waves are viridian, hanging low and large, thumping slowly down in champagne froth and lacy spray. The otters play through the foam and surf with such unfettered joy that we know, even in moments of doubt, that spring is on its way.

In February such gentle days are brief. Winds soon return: 'It's not time yet!' they shout, 'not time yet for spring!' No sweet murmurations here: birds are hurled about and, with skill and heart-bursting endeavour, they soar up only to be tossed across the fields like old, dry leaves.

But slowly, steadily, light grows in strength, and there comes a day when it finds the nooks and crannies of the fields, sneaking in between tree trunks and delving into shadowy recesses in byre and croft house. And suddenly a golden glow filters deep through retinas into minds, so bodies shift, heads lift, hearts beat more swiftly, lungs fill, change is sensed.

Soon longer, mad March days arrive with lofty bright blueness and energetic risings of thin white clouds. White-topped, sparkling waves call out to one another, and in their headlong rush to the shore whip up fizzy delights, cappuccino foam. In the dunes, machair grasses nod and dance, trying to catch the breezes. Above the whirling of air and waves comes the sound of joyous voices, euphoric, unrestrained: the first skylarks are pitching lungs, hearts and minds in unison with the sea.

Other pre-equinoctial days are not so effervescent and succumb to biting cold, icy crystals and glistening beads of snow and hail. There is a lowness to the landscape then: across the fields, the tufted grasses are still bleached blonde and sodden, heathers gnarled and frizzled to burnt umber and remnants of bronze bracken fronds are scattered here and there. And yet this squishy, pale mat of grass is gradually being absorbed back into the slowly warming earth, its job of protecting soil, fungi, bacteria, worms and hibernating insect larvae during winter now done. Here and there bright green shards appear like livid swords, piercing the mesh and tangle. In this still-dampened-down world, little pathways are visible: Lilliputian highways and low-ways for secret furry scurryings; neat spiralled entrances to dew-covered, spider-webbed dens, some only a finger's width, thresholds to the undergrass byways of voles, shrews and mice, safe from raptor camera-lens vision.

Above, another highway: gulls and terns gather and bustle, shouting their greetings in the early morning airs as they follow the same route along the river as it meanders through the croft fields down to the sea, like a school run. They gather on the glistening sands or bouncing waves, shrieking and clamouring, organising last year's youngsters in frowzy brown and grey groups. And when the business is done, the register complete, up they soar to follow other indiscernible airy trails.

But soon there comes a day when a heart-warming yellowness spreads across the croft land. Not the pale bleachings of winter and not yet the vibrant, vernal greens of full spring. A sudden yellowing. Lemon ice-cream mist and melon-gold haze. A gift of warmth and sun has tickled awake marzipan-scented gorse flowers and creamy catkins. Suddenly there are yellows everywhere: sunlight is illuminating fuzzy pineapple-yellow bumblebee bottoms, golden-breasted songbirds and grapefruit-yellow cowslips.

At the woodland edges, the royal purple finery of birch branches is slowly being replaced by livid lime brightness. Winter-bare larch branches are being outfitted in bushy costumes as needled tresses sprout in jade and green and, at last, the solemn brown buds of ancient oak trees are opening, burnishing branch tips lightly and joyously in copper. On the peaty moorland, dark russet and chocolate stems of bog myrtle are painted bright orange as their flowers burst open with scents so fragrant and resinous that they are at once uplifting and healing.

In the heady, scented airs and currents, even when this lemon posset of spring newness is hurled about yet again by biting winds and snow flurries, the sap-rising rush of change is upon us, light-impelled, undeterred. And, above it all, the choruses of larks and cuckoos, undaunted by the frowning, still-winter-white-tipped mountains. Spring has arrived in the Highlands.

Annie Worsley, 2016

Before the swallow, before the daffodil, and not much later than the snowdrop, the common toad salutes the coming of spring after his own fashion, which is to emerge from a hole in the ground, where he has lain buried since the previous autumn, and crawl as rapidly as possible towards the nearest suitable patch of water. Something – some kind of shudder in the earth, or perhaps merely a rise of a few degrees in the temperature – has told him that it is time to wake up: though a few toads appear to sleep the clock round and miss out a year from time to time – at any rate, I have more than once dug them up, alive and apparently well, in the middle of the summer.

At this period, after his long fast, the toad has a very spiritual look, like a strict Anglo-Catholic towards the end of Lent. His movements are languid but purposeful, his body is shrunken, and by contrast his eyes look abnormally large. This allows one to notice, what one might not at another time, that a toad has about the most beautiful eye of any living creature. It is like gold, or more exactly it is like the golden-coloured semi-precious stone which one sometimes sees in signet-rings, and which I think is called a chrysoberyl.

For a few days after getting into the water the toad concentrates on building up his strength by eating small insects. Presently he has swollen to his normal size again, and then he goes through a phase of intense sexiness. All he knows, at least if he is a male toad, is that he wants to get his arms round something, and if you offer him a stick, or even your finger, he will cling to it with surprising strength and take a long time to discover that it is not a female toad. Frequently one comes upon shapeless masses of ten or twenty toads rolling over and over in the water, one clinging to another without distinction of sex. By degrees, however, they sort themselves out into couples, with the male duly sitting on the female's back. You can now distinguish males from females, because the male is smaller, darker and sits on top, with his arms tightly clasped round the female's neck. After a day or two the spawn is laid in long strings which wind themselves in and out of the reeds and soon become invisible. A few more weeks, and the water is alive with masses of tiny tadpoles which rapidly grow larger, sprout hind-legs, then forelegs, then shed their tails: and finally, about the middle of the summer, the new generation of toads, smaller than one's thumb-nail but perfect in every particular, crawl out of the water to begin the game anew.

I mention the spawning of the toads because it is one of the phenomena of spring which most deeply appeal to me, and because the toad, unlike the skylark and the primrose, has never had much of a boost from poets. But I am aware that many people do not like reptiles or amphibians, and I am not suggesting that in order to enjoy the spring you have to take an interest in toads. There are also the crocus, the missel-thrush, the cuckoo, the blackthorn, etc. The point is that the pleasures of spring are available to everybody, and cost nothing. Even in the most sordid street the coming of spring will register itself by some sign or other, if it is only a brighter blue between the chimney pots or the vivid green of an elder sprouting on a blitzed site. Indeed it is remarkable how Nature goes on existing unofficially, as it were, in the very heart of London. I have seen a kestrel flying over the Deptford gasworks, and I have heard a first-rate performance by a blackbird in the Euston Road. There must be some hundreds of thousands, if not millions, of birds living inside the four-mile radius, and it is rather a pleasing thought that none of them pays a halfpenny of rent.

As for spring, not even the narrow and gloomy streets round the Bank of England are quite able to exclude it. It comes seeping in everywhere, like one of those new poison gases which pass through all filters. The spring is commonly referred to as 'a miracle', and during the past five or six years this worn-out figure of speech has taken on a new lease of life. After the sorts of winters we have had to endure recently, the spring does seem miraculous, because it has become gradually harder and harder to believe that it is actually going to happen. Every February since 1940 I have found myself thinking that this time winter is going to be permanent. But Persephone, like the toads, always rises from the dead at about the same moment. Suddenly, towards the end of March, the miracle happens and the decaying slum in which I live is transfigured. Down in the square the sooty privets have turned bright green, the leaves are thickening on the chestnut trees, the daffodils are out, the wallflowers are budding, the policeman's tunic looks positively a pleasant shade of blue, the fishmonger greets his customers with a smile, and even the sparrows are quite a different colour, having felt the balminess of the air and nerved themselves to take a bath, their first since last September.

Is it wicked to take a pleasure in spring and other seasonal changes? To put it more precisely, is it politically reprehensible, while we are all groaning, or at any rate ought to be groaning, under the shackles of the capitalist system, to point out that life is frequently more worth living because of a blackbird's song, a yellow elm tree in October, or some other natural phenomenon which does not cost money and does not have what the editors of left-wing newspapers call a class angle? There is no doubt that many people think so. I know by experience that a favourable reference to 'Nature' in one of my articles is liable to bring me abusive letters, and though the key-word in these letters is usually 'sentimental', two ideas seem to be mixed up in them. One is that any pleasure in the actual process of life encourages a sort of political quietism. People, so the thought runs, ought to be discontented, and it is our job to multiply our wants and not simply to increase our enjoyment of the things we have already. The other idea is that this is the age of machines and that to dislike the machine, or even to want to limit its domination, is backward-looking, reactionary and slightly ridiculous. This is often backed up by the statement that a love of Nature is a foible of urbanised people who have no notion what Nature is really like. Those who really have to deal with the soil, so it is argued, do not love the soil, and do not take the faintest interest in birds or flowers, except from a strictly utilitarian point of view. To love the country one must live in the town, merely taking an occasional week-end ramble at the warmer times of year.

This last idea is demonstrably false. Medieval literature, for instance, including the popular ballads, is full of an almost Georgian enthusiasm for Nature, and the art of agricultural peoples such as the Chinese and Japanese centre always round trees, birds, flowers, rivers, mountains. The other idea seems to me to be wrong in a subtler way. Certainly we ought to be discontented, we ought not simply to find out ways of making the best of a bad job, and yet if we kill all pleasure in the actual process of life, what sort of future are we preparing for ourselves? If a man cannot enjoy the return of spring, why should he be happy in a labour-saving Utopia? What will he do with the leisure that the machine will give him? I have always suspected that if our economic and political problems are ever really solved, life will become simpler instead of more complex, and that the sort of pleasure one gets from finding the first primrose will loom larger than the sort of pleasure one gets from eating an ice to the tune of a Wurlitzer. I think that by retaining one's childhood love of such things as trees, fishes, butterflies and – to return to my first instance – toads, one makes a peaceful and decent future a little more probable, and that by preaching the doctrine that nothing is to be admired except steel and concrete, one merely makes it a little surer that human beings will have no outlet for their surplus energy except in hatred and leader worship.

At any rate, spring is here, even in London N.1, and they can't stop you enjoying it. This is a satisfying reflection. How many a time have I stood watching the toads mating, or a pair of hares having a boxing match in the young corn, and thought of all the important persons who would stop me enjoying this if they could. But luckily they can't. So long as you are not actually ill, hungry, frightened or immured in a prison or a holiday camp, spring is still spring. The atom bombs are piling up in the factories, the police are prowling through the cities, the lies are streaming from the loudspeakers, but the earth is still going round the sun, and neither the dictators nor the bureaucrats, deeply as they disapprove of the process, are able to prevent it.

George Orwell, 'Some Thoughts on the Common Toad', 1946

February to March

Feb. 26. The ground is covered with snow. People that were abroad early say the cold was very intense. The ground was as hard as iron.

Feb. 29. [South Lambeth] Remarkable vivid Aurora borealis.

Mar. 6. [London] Sky-larks mount and sing.

Mar. 8. Mrs Snooke dyed, aged 86.

Mar. 12. [Ringmer] No turnips to be seen on the road.

Mar. 14. Chaffinches sing but in a shorter way than in Hants.

Mar. 15. Mrs Snooke was buried.

Mar. 17. [Dorking] Brought away Mrs Snooke's old tortoise, Timothy, which she valued much, & had treated kindly for near 40 years. When dug out of its hybernaculum, it resented the Insult by hissing.

Mar. 18. [Selborne] No turnips to be seen on the road. Green plovers [lapwings] on the common. The uncrested wren, the smallest species, called in this place the *Chif-chaf* is very loud in the Lythe. This is the earliest summer bird of passage, & the harbinger of spring. It has only two piercing notes.

Footnote. Thomas kept the quantity of rain in my absence. [Only two entries made]

Mar. 20. We took the tortoise out of its box & buried it in the garden: but the weather being warm it heaved up the mould, & walked twice down to the bottom of the long walk to survey the premises.

Mar. 21. The tortoise is quite awake, & came-out all day long: towards the evening it buried itself in part.

Mar. 25. Sowed carrots, parsneps, planted potatoes. Ground works well. Tortoise sleeps.

Mar. 28. The tortoise put-out his head in the morning.

Mar. 30. The tortoise keeps close.

Reverend Gilbert White, The Naturalist's Journal, *1780*

Next day the wind has flown and the snow is again almost rain: there is ever a hint of pale sky above, but it is not as luminous as the earth. The trees over the road have a beauty of darkness and moistness. Beyond them the earth is a sainted corpse, with a blue light over it that is fast annihilating all matter and turning the landscape to a spirit only. Night and the snow descend upon it, and at dawn the nests are full of snow. The yews and junipers on a league of Downs are chequered white upon white slopes, and the green larches support cirrus clouds of snow. In the garden the daffodils bend criss-cross under snow that cannot quite conceal the yellow flowers.

But the snow has ceased. The sky is at first pale without a cloud and tender as from a long imprisonment; it deepens in hue as the sun climbs and gathers force. The crooked paths up the Downs begin to glitter like streaks of lightning. The thrushes sing. From the straight dark beeches the snow cannot fall fast enough in great drops, in showers, in masses that release the boughs with a quiver and a gleam. The green leaves close to the ground creep out, and against them the snow is blue.

A little sighing wind rustles ivy and juniper and yew. The sun mounts, and from his highest battlement of cloud blows a long blast of light over the pure land. Once more the larch is wholly green, the beech rosy brown with buds. A cart goes by all a-gleam with a load of crimson-sprouting swedes and yellow-sprouting mangolds that seem to be burning through the net of snow above them. Down each side of every white road runs a stream that sings and glitters in ripples like innumerable crystal flowers. Water drips and trickles and leaps and gushes and oozes everywhere, and extracts the fragrance of earth and green and flowers under the heat that hastens to undo the work of the snow. The air is hot and wet. The snow is impatient to be water again. It still makes a cape over the briers and brambles, and there is a constant drip and steam and song of drops from the crossing branches in the cave below. Loud sounds the voice of leaf and branch and imprisoned water in the languor and joy of their escape. On every hand there is a drip and gush and ooze of water, a crackle and rustle and moan of plants and trees unfolding and unbending and greeting air and light; a close, humid, many-perfumed host; wet gloom and a multitudinous glitter; a movement of water and of the shadows like puffs of smoke that fleet over the white fields under the clouds.

And over and through it a cuckoo is crying and crying, first overhead, then afar, and gradually near and retreating again. He is soon gone, but the ears are long afterwards able to extract the spirit of the song, the exact interval of it, from among all the lasting sounds, until we hear it as clearly as before, out of the blue sky, out of the white cloud, out of the shining grey water. It is a word of power – cuckoo! The melting of the snow is faster than ever, and at the end of the day there is none left except in some hollows of the Downs on the slopes behind the topmost of the beeches that darkly fringe the violet sky. In the misty shutting of the light there are a thousand songs laced by cuckoos' cries and the first hooting of owls, and the beeches have become merely straight lines of pearl in a mist of their own boughs.

Below them, in the high woods, goes on the fall of the melting snow through the gloomy air, and the splash on the dead leaves. This gloom and monotonous sound make an exquisite cloister, visited but not disturbed by the sound of the blackbirds singing in the mist of the vale underneath. Slowly the mist has deepened from the woods to the vale and now the eye cannot see from tree to tree.

Then the straight heavy rain descends upon the songs and the clatterings of blackbirds, and when they are silenced the moorhen's watery hoot announces that the world belongs to the beasts and the rainy dark until tomorrow.

Beautiful upon the waters, beautiful upon the mountains, is the cuckoo's song, and most rare over the snow.

But of all places and hours I should choose the crags of Land's End in a dawn of June; and let it be the end of that month and the wind be grey and cold, so that the ships stagger in the foam and crag-like waves as they catch the early light tenderly upon their sails. The cold beams, the high precipices yet full of shadow and of the giddy calling of daw and gull, the black but white-lipped water and the blacker cormorant flying straight across it just over the foam, the sky golden yet still pallid and trembling from the dungeon of night – through it floats that beloved voice breaking, breaking, and the strong year at the summit of its career has begun to decline.

The song is memorable and fair also when the drenched gardens toss and spread their petals in the grass. Many a one hears it who will not hear it again, and many that once expected it impatiently hears it no more because he is old and deaf or because his heart is closed. There is not a broad and perfect day of heat and wind and sunshine that is not haunted by that voice seeming to say the earth is hollow under our feet and the sky hollow over our heads.

There are whole nights when the cuckoo will not sleep, and the woods on either side of a road twenty miles long emit the cry of these conquerors under the full moon and the white stars of love. If you pause it will appear that it is not a silence that this song rules over; for what was a silence was full of sounds, as many sounds as there are leaves, sounds of creeping, gliding, pattering, rustling, slow wormlike continuous noises and sudden sounds. And strangely at length is the glorious day reared high upon the ruins of this night, of which the survivors slink away into the old forgotten roads, the dense woods, the chimneys of deserted houses.

It is a jolly note only when the bird is visible close at hand and the power of his throat is felt. Often two or three will answer one another, or for half a day will loiter about a coombe for the sake of an echo. It is one of the richest sounds in nature when two sing together, the second note of one being almost blended with the first of the other; and so they continue as if themselves entranced by the harmony, and the navvy leans upon his pick to listen.

On the day after the great melting of the snow the white beam tree, at the edges of high woods and in the midst of the beeches, has its hour, when its thousands of large white buds point upward like a multitudinous candelabrum. For me the white beam is always associated with wayfaring. Its white buds are the traveller's joy of spring. The buds like blossoms or flames bewitch from afar off. They are always upon sloping ground and usually upon hillsides in the chalk land. In the autumn their leaves often shrivel before falling, and turn to a colour that looks like pink almond blossom by contrast with juniper and yew. When they have fallen, they are as much to be noticed. They lie commonly with their white undersides uppermost, and though rain soaks them and wind scatters them and they are trodden down, they preserve their whiteness until the winter or the following spring. It is a tree that belongs, above all others except the yew, to the Pilgrims' Way, and it is impossible to forget these leaves lying white on the untouched wayside sward, among the dewy purple and crimson and gold of other leaves, sparkling in the sun and entering into all the thoughts and fancies and recollections that come to one who goes in solitude along that old road when the scent of the dying year is pungent as smoke and sweet as flowers.

Edward Thomas, The South Country, *1909*

Primrose

The desire for you is hidden
no creature feathered, bare
or fur-footed knows
without the lengthening of days
what you are

when a bee knows it's a bee
it stops questioning
the purpose of its life

how soon the keen gardener
recognises what was planted
but this is early spring

the air is free of fervent hums
and what is poking through
the broken ground
could be anything

Shamshad Khan, 2016

The frost held for many weeks, until the birds were dying rapidly. Everywhere in the fields and under the hedges lay the ragged remains of lapwings, starlings, thrushes, redwings, innumerable ragged bloody cloaks of birds, whence the flesh was eaten by invisible beasts of prey.

Then, quite suddenly, one morning, the change came. The wind went to the south, came off the sea warm and soothing. In the afternoon there were little gleams of sunshine, and the doves began, without interval, slowly and awkwardly to coo. The doves were cooing, though with a laboured sound, as if they were still winter-stunned. Nevertheless, all the afternoon they continued their noise, in the mild air, before the frost had thawed off the road. At evening the wind blew gently, still gathering a bruising quality of frost from the hard earth. Then, in the yellow-gleamy sunset, wild birds began to whistle faintly in the blackthorn thickets of the stream-bottom.

It was startling and almost frightening, after the heavy silence of frost. How could they sing at once, when the ground was thickly strewn with the torn carcases of birds? Yet out of the evening came the uncertain, silvery sounds that made one's soul start alert, almost with fear. How could the little silver bugles sound the rally so swiftly, in the soft air, when the earth was yet bound? Yet the birds continued their whistling, rather dimly and brokenly, but throwing the threads of silver, germinating noise into the air.

It was almost a pain to realise, so swiftly, the new world.

Le monde est morte. Vive le monde! But the birds omitted even the first part of the announcement, their cry was only a faint, blind, fecund '*vive!*'

There is another world. The winter is gone. There is a new world of spring. The voice of the turtle is heard in the land. But the flesh shrinks from so sudden a transition. Surely the call is premature, while the clods are still frozen, and the ground is littered with the remains of wings! Yet we have no choice. In the bottoms of impenetrable blackthorn, each evening and morning now, out flickers a whistling of birds.

Where does it come from, the song? After so long a cruelty, how can they make it up so quickly? But it bubbles through them, they are like little well-heads, little fountain-heads whence the spring trickles and bubbles forth. It is not of their own doing. In their throats new life distils itself into sound. It is the rising of the silvery sap of a new summer, gurgling itself forth.

All the time, whilst the earth lay choked and killed and winter-mortified, the deep undersprings were quiet. They only wait for the ponderous encumbrance of the old order to give way, yield in the thaw, and there they are, a silver realm at once. Under the surge of ruin, unmitigated winter, lies the silver potentiality of all blossom. One day the black tide must spend itself and fade back. Then all-suddenly appears the crocus, hovering triumphant in the rear, and we know the order has changed, there is a new régime, sound of a new *Vive! vive!*

It is no use any more to look at the torn remnants of birds that lie exposed. It is no longer any use remembering the sullen thunder of frost and the intolerable pressure of cold upon us. For whether we will or not, they are gone. The choice is not ours. We may remain wintry and destructive for a little longer, if we wish it, but the winter is gone out of us, and willy-nilly our hearts sing a little at sunset.

Even whilst we stare at the ragged horror of birds scattered broadcast, part-eaten, the soft, uneven cooing of the pigeon ripples from the outhouses, and there is a faint silver whistling in the bushes come twilight. No matter, we stand and stare at the torn and unsightly ruins of life, we watch the weary, mutilated columns of winter retreating under our eyes. Yet in our ears are the silver vivid bugles of a new creation advancing on us from behind, we hear the rolling of the soft and happy drums of the doves.

We may not choose the world. We have hardly any choice for ourselves. We follow with our eyes the bloody and horrid line of march of this extreme winter, as it passes away. But we cannot hold back the spring. We can make the birds silent, prevent the bubbling of the wood pigeons. We cannot stay the fine world of silver-fecund creation from gathering itself and taking place upon us. Whether we will or no, the daphne tree will soon be giving off perfume, the lambs dancing on two feet, the celandines will twinkle all over the ground, there will be new heaven and new earth.

For it is in us, as well as without us. Those who can may follow the columns of winter in their retreat from off the earth. Some of us, we have no choice, the spring is within us, the silver fountain begins to bubble under our breast, there is gladness in spite of ourselves. And on the instant we accept the gladness! The first day of change, out whistles an unusual, interrupted paean, a fragment that will augment itself imperceptibly. And this in spite of the extreme bitterness of the suffering, in spite of the myriads of torn dead.

Such a long, long winter and the frost only broke yesterday. Yet it seems, already, we cannot remember it. It is strangely remote, like a far-off darkness. It is as unreal as a dream in the night. This is the morning of reality, when we are ourselves. This natural and real, the glimmering of a new creation that stirs in us and about us. We know there was winter, long, fearful. We know the earth was strangled and mortified, we know the body of life was torn and scattered broadcast. But what is this retrospective knowledge? It is something extraneous to us, extraneous to this that we are now. And what we are, and what, it seems, we always have been, is this quickening lovely silver plasm of pure creativity. All the mortification and tearing, ah yes, it was upon us, encompassing us. It was like a storm or a mist or a falling from a height. It was entangled upon us, like bats in our hair, driving us mad. But it was never really our innermost self. Within, we were always apart, we were this, this limpid fountain of silver, then quiescent, rising and breaking now into the flowering.

It is strange, the utter incompatibility of death with life. Whilst there is death, life is not to be found. It is all death, one overwhelming flood. And then a new tide rises, and it is all life, a fountain of silvery blissfulness. It is one or the other. We are for life, or we are for death, one or the other, but never in our essence both at once.

Death takes us, and all is a torn redness, passing into darkness. Life rises, and we are faint fine jets of silver running out to blossom. All is incompatible with all. There is the silvery-speckled, incandescent-lovely thrush, whistling pipingly his first song in the blackthorn thicket. How is he to be connected with the bloody, feathered unsightliness of thrush-remnants just outside the bushes? There is no connection. They are not to be referred the one to the other. Where one is, the other is not. In the kingdom of death the silvery song is not. But where there is life, there is no death. No death whatever, only silvery gladness, perfect, the otherworld.

The blackbird cannot stop his song, neither can the pigeon. It takes place in him, even though all his race was yesterday destroyed. He cannot mourn, or be silent, or adhere to the dead. Of the dead he is not, since life has kept him. The dead must bury their dead. Life has now taken hold on him and tossed him into the new ether of a new firmament, where he bursts into song as if he were combustible. What is the past, those others, now he is tossed clean into the new, across the untranslatable difference?

In his song is heard the first brokenness and uncertainty of the transition. The transit from the grip of death into new being is a death from death, in its sheer metempsychosis a dizzy agony. But only for a second, the moment of trajectory, the passage from one state to the other, from the grip of death to the liberty of newness. In a moment he is in the kingdom of wonder, singing at the centre of a new creation.

The bird did not hang back. He did not cling to his death and his dead. There is no death, and the dead have buried their dead. Tossed into the chasm between the two worlds, he lifted his wings in dread, and found himself carried on the impulse.

We are lifted to be cast away into the new beginning. Under our hearts the fountain surges, to toss us forth. Who can thwart the impulse that comes upon us? It comes from the unknown upon us, and it behoves us to pass delicately and exquisitely upon the subtle new wind from heaven, conveyed like birds in unreasoning migration from death to life.

D. H. Lawrence, 'Whistling of Birds', 1919

Snowdrops are well known little white flowers, which indicate the first return of spring. The early Catholics in monastery gardens, who first named most of our plants, called them Our Lady of February, from their first opening about the feast of the Purification or Candlemas Day. This became more corrupted into Fair Maid of February. They continue to blow till March.

Thomas Furly Forster, The Pocket Encyclopaedia of Natural Phenomena, *published 1827*

The water is shattered by ripples as I approach the pond: a flock of small ducks has exploded away. I make a quick count: nine mandarins. They are exotic escapees, here to stay, and here to breed. Alder Carr, my secret woodland place since childhood, is perfect for them. Swampy and inaccessible, it is full of leaning, falling, hollow trees to nest in.

It's a dark day at the beginning of March. The trees reflected in the water are upside down, all the life shaken out of them. I used to find winter trees depressing, they seemed such gothic skeletons – but I was not the kind of girl who wanted to paint her bedroom black, and I grew to love them. Now I wait for the seasons to decorate them with the white iron-filings of hoar frost, with stencilled flocks of fieldfares, with the catkins so teasingly described by Birkin in D. H. Lawrence's *Women in Love*. The black tracery of winter trees will give way to leaf-buds that unfurl in a drench of chlorophyll, and seem to host all the birds of the air as migrants arrive in surges and falls. Warblers from Africa, tiny birds as elegant as the leaves, will perch among them, pick off insects and begin their songs.

I look closer. Tiny animated dots on the twigs draw my eyes to the tops of the alders. I tune into the clamorous twitter of squeaking silhouettes. Without binoculars I think, *siskins*. When I put the glasses to my eyes I breathe deeper, knowing for sure. I see a single duck feather in the water. It is curled and buoyant in its sheen of grease. Every filament reflects light and colour. Adrift, it seems to belong in this element with as much life as a swimming bird.

Next day, I have to face the news. We drive over the hill to where the incinerator chimney of Addenbrooke's Hospital insults us with its usual rude gesture. I find the hospital's corridors so confusing, I've sometimes lost my temper here. Do staff and patients ever get to know it like the backs of their hands, like the animals that tread the same path night after night: a highway to a meal, or an escape route? On the new estate beyond the hospital I once saw a hare dash purposefully into a cul-de-sac that simply wasn't there a few months before. In the clinic I hear murmurs of fear and patience and complaint. I receive loud, rude, brusquely scientific and kindly insistent words.

I bide my time as winter endures. Walking through thick, low cloud I can hear spring. There are skylarks high above. I see a smidgeon of yellow, budgie-bright: a yellowhammer sings a childhood rhyme. There's a single pair of lapwings on the heavy clay plough land, plaintively defending their eggs from the crows.

Spring light shines and dims. Lambs drop warm from the womb and lie tucked up in rain and hail. Long-tailed tits begin to spring-clean the exterior of our house, collecting the gossamer threads of spider webs to weave an elastic, mossy dome, lined with 2,000 feathers and concealed with lichen. But such an early nest does not have the benefit of leaves on the trees for camouflage. I find it ripped from its mooring, emptied by a predator.

Violets (my favourites) appear. I get down and inhale the brief, potent, ionine scent. I do this every year, but I no longer murmur the names that spring inspired: *Violet, Sylvi, Eleanor, Leonie, Esther, Jay*. I walk up the hill out of the village to open farmland where mile upon mile of intensive agriculture lies upon ancient settlements below. Channels have been drilled for potatoes. The freshly turned soil is warmer than the frosty air; white horses of mist gallop along each furrow.

I am put under the knife. Immediately after the operation we have the warmest, brightest April. I have three weeks' recuperation. I get the chance to sit back and watch spring do its thing in amazing detail. It is pretty. It is Walt Disney. It is murderous.

Birds in plush spring plumage criss-cross the garden, intent on courtship flights and chases. Mostly I watch unseen. Two robins fight frenziedly. Their squawks are furious and terrified. I watch the weaker bird get wedged under a wooden panel as it flees. The victor starts to peck it to death, and I intervene. Tree-creepers spiral up the silver birches in a scratchy, ponderous dance. A male kingfisher attracts a female to a perch. Over and over again he offers her a fish. For a while she maintains an oddly stiff and stubborn stance. I watch until she accepts the gift.

The pond is heaving with amphibians and ducks. Gross knots and balls of male toads bob about, clasping a single female. A female mallard can't escape the drakes. They chase her through sky and water, and they chase her when she dives.

I step quietly towards the frogs, but they make themselves invisible as soon as I approach. There are already clumps of jelly, bulbous and resilient and fresh, protecting thousands of eggs. I touch the cold jelly with two fingers, and realise I don't really mind it all carrying on without me. There was a time when seeing an act of mothering made me weep.

I have witnessed a mallard duck drowning a rat to protect her brood. I've seen a doe rabbit attacking a stoat. For years it seemed as though nature was getting on with it perfectly successfully, and I was the odd one out. But of course wild lives are as precarious as they are strong. The natural world I observe is merciless, but it's a place where I feel happy to belong.

Jo Sinclair, 2016

First Milk

Today I carried a newborn lamb
hung by his hooves,
over the farm gate,
into the deep straw manger I had made.

And there I made my first mistake,
I named him:
'Hello Waldorf' I whispered,
and sprayed blue paint on his wet woolly back,
still steaming in the cold March air.

In the next makeshift bed
pallets were bound with old twine rope,
nets of hay hung from a rust hook,
and Waldorf's mother bleated for him.

I crept up behind the ewe,
rolled her onto her back,
and pulled at the sore swollen teats
until they fired hot savage spurts of colostrum
into my Pyrex jar.

With my plastic syringe
I dribbled the first milk

onto my wrist
and gripped Waldorf between my legs,
head-locking him
until he gagged
from my surrogate pipe.

I wrapped him up in a muddy blanket,
dipped iodine on his umbilical cord,
held him close, my triplet runt,
and pretended my heartbeat
would send him to sleep.

Adelle Stripe, 2012

A band of woodland cloaks the slope up to the brow of Newtimber Hill. At the top it opens out on to chalk downland. I am walking today and the light is lemon clear, the sun, taut as a drum, stretched tight across the sky. There is a refreshing nip in the early spring air; I can see my breath.

The path meanders through the trees then climbs towards a gate. The sun greets me in a full, warming glow. I bask for a few moments; there is a joy to being in the woods at the start of spring. As a child I came to this same hillside – Sunday afternoons, duffle coat, mitts, red cheeks; that old duffle coat like the slopes now felted green.

The wood descends in a cross-hatch of branches scratched and inked in with rooks' nests. Before me, undulating downland, peppered with dandelion, hawkbit and birds-foot trefoil. All is harmonious, humming with new life.

Then I see a movement, a sudden squiggle of a movement along the woodland edge. Squirrel? It is the colour of a dull penny, the russet of autumn, a creature out of season here to tease me; stoat. Long, perky, berry-eyed, his lightness unsettles me. I waiver mid-stride, unsteady on the slope, hoping not to make a sound. I see the black-tipped tail as the stoat wriggles along a line of scent like a toy pulled by a string. He hesitates, tastes the air and then, with fluid deliberation, bounds down the hill into the bramble and old man's beard.

I stand mesmerised. At my feet a bee-fly inspects the close-cropped turf of an anthill, her proboscis needle-sharp, wings a fuzz of air. I smile and walk on, following the stoat's trail, sure that I will not see him again. But I'm wrong. Out of the brambles the stoat shoots in hot pursuit of a baby rabbit, a ball of beige, wholemeal pastry before it's cooked. I bite my lip, wince. They disappear and the tangle of stems quivers and squeals.

But it is not over yet. A few moments later, from the thorny stems the stoat flees, pursued by the largest of rabbits – almost the size of a hare – hard on his tail. Soft fur and muscle, hind legs thundering, the vibration of rage. Giant rabbit after small stoat, down the slope they go, the impudence of the stoat overwhelmed by the fury of his prey.

It is, perhaps, no surprise that the stoat ventured out so bold this early spring day. A young stoat, overconfident, hungry, perhaps lacking in skill. Today he has learnt something. There is no sign of the young rabbit; it escaped to live for now. All is well in the world of rabbit.

A raft of cloud crosses the sky, teased out over the drum of the sun as a green woodpecker whoops over, sewing the air between down and wood with invisible thread. I continue along the path towards the light.

Alexi Francis, 2016

In early spring, before there is much spreading of leaf or opening of flower in the woods and lanes, there is a good deal to be seen in and around an old pond. By an *old* pond, I mean one that I have known for years: one that does not dry up in summer, though it may then have less water and a broader shore. To-day it is very full, owing to the snow and rain of winter; but the water is very clear, for the leaves that almost filled it in autumn have all decayed and gone to form that fine mud at the bottom in which so many small living things find food and a home.

The great screen of Reeds at one end of the pond, that keeps up a steady rustle as the wind shakes it, is showing little sign of life; but if you look down among the dead stems you will see many new green shoots showing in the shallow water. The Reed is the largest of all the British grasses; it has a way of sending out shoots in to the water from which new stems arise; and after a time the pond will get filled up by it, and we shall have to look for a fresh hunting place. The big blackish bird with the red forehead that has rushed out from among the Reeds with a loud cry of 'cur-ruck' is the Moorhen. Probably there is a nest hidden there.

Under the Reed-shoots, and in the mud at the bottom, may forms of pond-life have passed the winter quietly, but are now active again, some of them making up for a long fast. The grown-up Frogs that in autumn buried themselves in the mud, woke up in March and set about the laying of eggs in the pond. Though at first these were very small, they soaked up so much water that they soon became as big as peas, each a ball of clear jelly with a darker, solid centre which we may call the yolk of the egg, its most important part.

These eggs – of which one Frog produces a thousand or more – are soft and sticky, and all cling together in a great mass which now floats at the surface of the water. If we are able to watch them day by day, we shall find that the blackish yolks soon begin to lengthen. A good plan is to take home a small portion of the jelly-mass and place it in a pan of water, with some fresh pond-weed, so that we can watch the changes closely. We shall see the yolk become long and narrow; soon we can make out which end will be the head, though when the head is formed, at first it has neither eyes nor a mouth. But it shows that the germ is alive; and a day or two later is gets outside of the jelly and clings to its surface. Then eyes and mouth and gills appear, head and body joined are finished off by a long tail, and we get near to the proper Tadpole form. The little animals grow rapidly; so that, when a large number have left the jelly-mass and are swimming in the clear water, the pond appears to be full of Tadpoles.

At this stage of growth, they are much like fishes, for they breathe by means of gills which extract air from the water; they swim like fishes by rapid movements of the tail from side to side. As they grow larger they lose the fish form: the head and body become round and a pair of tiny hind-legs breaks out from the base of the tail. The front pair is coming also; but at present these legs are under cover and do not show. Then, as the legs grow and get strong enough to use, the tail becomes smaller, and by and by is not there. It has not dropped off, as some people will tell you it does, but has been absorbed into the body. The gills go also; and the young hopping Frog now breathes through its nostrils and lungs as we do. For a time, it will hide among the damp grass and weeds near the pond, and wait for heavy rain, when it will feel that it is safe to go farther away in search of a moist corner where it can find plenty of insects to serve it for food.

Edward Step, Nature Rambles: An Introduction to Country-lore, *1930*

Highfield

As the footstep crackling, winter retreat ends,
the blackthorn shows its warrior nature.
White blossom speckles
its dark skeleton like stars,
which brave the still and frosty dawn.
The dog trots and sniffs, trots and sniffs,
raising a paw to combat
chilly steps.
Muzzle nudging dank, over-wintered leaves
reveal a snowdrop's green shoot,
a tentative finger raised
to test the air, still unsure.
A robin hops, whispers on a branch,
inconceivably close.
Orange light appears on this daybreak,
the colour of warmth, bringing hope
and a glimpse of future days.
At this time, it opens the mind to
the possibility of Spring.
The imagination warms and heads
groundwards where leaf mulch
gives way to humus and then cold soil.
The bulbs, stirring from the
warmth held deeper,

sense a new feeling in the wind
and are compelled to meet with it,
shrugging off the cool,
earthy layer for
new life and the welcoming air.
The tree has
wisdom in its roots,
tapping deep into the warming subsoil,
tuning into the core.
Bare branches reach forth, testing the sky,
talking to their roots
which tell sap to rise.
A surge begins in every plant
and beneath my feet I can feel
the ground awaken.
Spring is a silent dawn
which should roar
into life
as winter's night passes.

Alan Creedon, 2016

Snow storms again, and Hay Fair.

At 5 o'clock I went up the Bron and by the field path to little Wern y Pentre. The old people talked over some of the parish tragedies which I have heard of, the supposed murder of Price of Cwmrafan by Burton, his would-be son-in-law, by day on the high road near Cabalva, and the digging up of Jane Whitcombe's baby at the Bronith, a baby which was supposed to have met with foul play. 'It's bad to get them,' said old Williams shaking his head, 'but it's worse to do away with them.'

When I rose to go the snow was still falling thickly in enormous feathers and was growing deep upon the ground. I had not brought an umbrella and kind Mrs. Williams insisted upon my having her shawl to put over my shoulders. What kindly people these are. The leaden sky was awfully dark and low and seemed loaded with snow. I went down by the fields and wandered over the fields wide of the stiles, so much in a few minutes had the snow changed the look of everything. The sheep and lambs were running about in confusion crying piteously and all taken aback by the sudden storm. When I got to Penllan I could not help being struck by the change in the village. I had left it bright and sunny and green smiling under a blue sky. Now [after] an hour and a half it lay apparently deep in snow, snow on the village roofs, snow on the Church and Churchyard, snow on the green trees, snow everywhere. And over the village stooped low the terrible black leaden sky like a pall drooping lower and lower. Nothing could be more dark and dreary and depressing. But the trees were a beautiful sight. They were loaded thick with soft feathery snow in the most fairylike and fantastic shapes.

Monday, Lady Day [25 March 1871]

Reverend Francis Kilvert, Kilvert's Diary 1870–79

Lady's Wood in Cambridgeshire is a Wildlife Trust reserve and my nearest woodland. Each spring I watch as the plants and trees that have endured frosty nights and thin, crisp blankets of snow begin their cycle again, with a burst of new growth and fresh leaves to gather the life-giving sunlight. Animals that have slept through the cold winter begin to emerge, birds start to sing and invertebrates that have lain dormant in sheltered nooks venture forth in search of food.

Even on a chilly February day there is life to be found if you look closely enough. The bare twigs of a hazel in the understorey show tight leaf-buds closely wrapped in rosy sheaths no bigger than grains of rice. Among the twigs a tiny drinker moth caterpillar sits nestled out of the wind. It will have hatched last year and spent the winter in a torpid state, awaiting the green flush of spring leaves to continue growing before it can pupate.

The last stragglers of the fieldfare flocks that came here for the winter are picking at shrivelled hawthorn berries. A family troupe of long-tailed tits are joined by blue tits in their search for insects in the treetops. Apart from the fieldfares' occasional chatter and the peeping of the tits as they move through the wood, there isn't much sound other than the breeze in the branches above.

Mosses, lichens and glossy ivy leaves, winding their way around the tree trunks, are just about the only colour amongst the muted winter tones. As the weeks pass, the darker shades will gain vibrancy and new hues will be added to nature's palette.

By March there is a definite change in the atmosphere. A yellowhammer on the edge of the wood flashes golden in the pale sun, spooked by my presence. I note the first few vivid-green leaf-buds bursting on the hawthorn and a seven-spot ladybird ambling about amongst them. It isn't so silent now either; a wren trills its crystalline tune from the undergrowth and a robin's creamy melody floats down from a branch overhanging the path. Looking around on hearing the cough of a muntjac, I see its white tail bobbing as it bounds away between the trees.

High above, a grey squirrel leaps across the divide between one tree and another with a small crash. Although they don't hibernate fully like other species, grey squirrels tend to stay tucked up in leaf-lined dreys throughout the coldest spells and only emerge on milder winter days to raid their larders. As the weather improves and their stores dwindle they will turn to eating bark and leaf-buds.

The rich, earthy tones of winter have almost gone now. In their place is a carpet of green, interspersed with the odd clump of buttery yellow primroses, dainty purple violets and an occasional delicate white wood anemone, just opening. These are the first of many flowers that will take advantage of the spring sunshine while it can still reach the woodland floor through the bare canopy.

April is when Lady's Wood achieves its magnificent glory. It is a sensory overload of wonderful things. The stars of the floral show have begun to bloom: bluebells take the stage. In Lady's Wood they are particularly spectacular as they form an almost complete carpet. In places it is a pure, unbroken blue, like a cloudless summer sky; elsewhere the bluebells become part of a rich mosaic, with greater stitchwort and herb-Robert adding flecks of white and pink. The scent is extraordinary too: sweet and heady, especially in the early evening. At this time of day you might be lucky enough to find a hedgehog snuffling around in the undergrowth or glimpse a fox slinking off in search of its next meal.

Another sure sign that spring is here at last are the many insects buzzing around the flowers. Early bumblebees in search of nectar from the bluebells bend the already nodding flower heads even further towards the ground. On warm days they are joined by the first butterflies of the year, orange tips that flutter into the glades in search of Jack-by-the-hedge on which to lay their eggs.

The pond in the centre of the wood is now host to its annual influx of smooth newts which breed here. From the dead branch of a tree on the opposite side of the wood a great spotted woodpecker drums. Our seasonal visitors have started to arrive for the summer too: one of the first is the chiffchaff, a small brown warbler which declares its presence loudly from the treetops by singing its name repeatedly. It won't be long now until it is joined by cuckoos, swallows and a host of others.

The promise of sunshine that was whispered at first grows stronger with the lengthening days. Spring will ease into summer and the blaze of colour in the wood will soon be replaced with a tapestry of green as the trees take over once more. The blue will fade as yellow oilseed rape blooms in the fields beyond, and the flurry of activity that signified spring's arrival will gather pace as summer progresses and the breeding season begins.

Alice Hunter, 2016

The Seafarer (Old English)

Bearwas blostmum nimað, byrig fægriað,
wongas wlitigað, woruld onetteð;
ealle þa gemoniað modes fusne
sefan to siþe, þam þe swa þenceð
on flodwegas feor gewitan.
Swylce geac monað geomran reorde,
singeð sumeres weard, sorge beodeð
bitter in breosthord. þæt se beorn ne wat,
esteadig secg, hwæt þa sume dreogað
þe þa wræclastas widost lecgað.
Forþon nu min hyge hweorfeð ofer hreþerlocan,
min modsefa mid mereflode
ofer hwæles eþel hweorfeð wide,
eorþan sceatas, cymeð eft to me
gifre ond grædig, gielleð anfloga,
hweteð on hwælweg hreþer unwearnum
ofer holma gelagu. Forþon me hatran sind
dryhtnes dreamas þonne þis deade lif,
læne on londe.

[The woods take on blossoms, towns become fair,
fields grow beautiful, the world hastens on;
all these things urge on the eager mind,
the spirit to the journey, in one who thinks to travel

far on the paths of the sea.
The cuckoo too gives warning with mournful voice,
summer's watchman sings, foretells sorrow,
bitter in the heart. Of this that man knows nothing,
the warrior blessed with wealth, what some endure
who furthest tread the paths of exile.
And so now my spirit roams beyond the confines of the heart,
my spirit over the sea-flood;
it wanders wide over the whale's home,
the expanse of the earth, and comes back to me
eager and greedy; the lone flier cries,
incites the heart to the whale's way, irresistible,
across the ocean's floods. And so to me
the joys of the Lord are warmer than this dead life,
lent on land.]

Anon., c. 975. Translation by Eleanor Parker, 2014.

First voice (Very softly):

To begin at the beginning:

It is spring, moonless night in the small town, starless and bible-black, the cobblestreets silent and the hunched, courters'-and-rabbits' wood limping invisible down to the sloeblack, slow, black, crowblack, fishingboat-bobbing sea. The houses are blind as moles (though moles see fine tonight in the snouting, velvet dingles) or blind as Captain Cat there in the muffled middle by the pump and the town clock, the shops in mourning, the Welfare Hall in widows' weeds. And all the people of the lulled and dumbfound town are sleeping now.

Hush, the babies are sleeping, the farmers, the fishers, the tradesmen and pensioners, cobbler, schoolteacher, postman and publican, the undertaker and the fancy woman, drunkard, dressmaker, preacher, policeman, the webfoot cocklewomen and the tidy wives. Young girls lie bedded soft or glide in their dreams, with rings and trousseaux, bridesmaided by glowworms down the aisles of the organplaying wood. The boys are dreaming wicked or of the bucking ranches of the night and the jolly, rodgered sea. And the anthracite statues of the horses sleep in the fields, and the cows in the byres, and the dogs in the wetnosed yards; and the cats nap in the slant corners or lope sly, streaking and needling, on the one cloud of the roofs.

You can hear the dew falling, and the hushed town breathing.

Only your eyes are unclosed, to see the black and folded town fast, and slow, asleep.

And you alone can hear the invisible starfall, the darkest-before-dawn minutely dewgrazed stir of the black, dab-filled sea where the Arethusa, the Curlew and the Skylark, Zanzibar, Rhiannon, the Rover, the Cormorant, and the Star of Wales tilt and ride.

Listen. It is night moving in the streets, the processional salt slow musical wind in Coronation Street and Cockle Row, it is the grass growing on Llareggub Hill, dewfall, starfall, the sleep of birds in Milk Wood.

Listen. It is night in the chill, squat chapel, hymning in bonnet and brooch and bombazine black, butterfly choker and bootlace bow, coughing like nannygoats, sucking mintoes, fortywinking hallelujah; night in the four-ale, quiet as a domino; in Ocky Milkman's loft like a mouse with gloves; in Dai Bread's bakery flying like black flour. It is tonight in Donkey Street, trotting silent, with seaweed on its hooves, along the cockled cobbles, past curtained fernpot, text and trinket, harmonium, holy dresser, watercolours done by hand, china dog and rosy tin teacaddy. It is night neddying among the snuggeries of babies.

Look. It is night, dumbly, royally winding through the Coronation cherry trees; going through the graveyard of Bethesda with winds gloved and folded, and dew doffed; tumbling by the Sailors Arms.

Time passes. Listen. Time passes.

Come closer now.

Only you can hear the houses sleeping in the streets in the slow deep salt and silent black, bandaged night. Only you can see, in the blinded bedrooms, the combs and petticoats over the chairs, the jugs and basins, the glasses of teeth, Thou Shalt Not on the wall, and the yellowing dickybird-watching pictures of the dead. Only you can hear and see, behind the eyes of the sleepers, the movements and countries and mazes and colours and dismays and rainbows and tunes and wishes and flight and fall and despairs and big seas of their dreams.

From where you are, you can hear their dreams.

Dylan Thomas, Under Milk Wood, *1954*

At 4.21 in the morning, the earth turns enough towards the light that the sky over the sea at Orford Ness begins to change. The darkness thins – slowly, slowly – shifting in shade from black to deepest blue, like Indian ink diluted drop by drop. A few yards from the shore, where swell meets shingle, a robin stirs in a hazel. It blinks and opens its throat. A blackbird follows; then a thrush. The birdsong grows by the minute, washing across Britain, fizzing, burbling and bubbling, spreading west, north and south over the still-black hedges, fields, woods and gardens like a bow-wave ahead of the coming dawn.

Fifteen minutes later it floods through Yorkshire and passes my window. A blackbird on the TV aerial of a terrace opposite threads its own thick, liquid notes into the air, waking me. I turn over and try to sleep again, but it's no good. Listening to the ripples of notes, my mind flits with nervous thoughts. In a few hours I will tell my dad that I am going to be a father.

We pull on our walking boots a little after eight o'clock, as arranged a week ago. Dad's car is parked up on the road beside the meadow and the old railway at the edge of town. 'It's a good time to be out,' he says, unbuckling his seatbelt. I'm not sure whether he means the hour or the point in the year, but he's right in both cases. It's early March and the promise of spring is everywhere. As he zips up his jacket and checks his camera, I breathe in the familiar smell of the slick, mossy trees that overgrow the sidings. Black branches reach into the silver morning; below are tangles of under-bramble, gloomy, brittle

– but there is a faint trace of warmth in the air too. The earth is shrugging off its exoskeleton; I sense the ground stirring. Spoon-shaped foxglove leaves push through the dead foliage. Hawthorn buds split as limbs run with fresh, green blood. Catkins hang from willows.

'Ready?' Dad asks. I turn and nod. How will he react? That's what's on my mind. It's all above board, respectable – my wife and I are married; we share a happy home – but our income is not what it could be. Should be, perhaps. Being a writer requires surrendering financial security and living commission to commission. It often feels like being in permanent suspension, permanently waiting for the barren season to turn into one of plenty. Dad knows this too, and I worry he is going to tell me that providing for a child is more important than any artistic endeavour. I worry he'll say it's time to knuckle down and find a safe job. Like he did. And I worry I won't be able to disagree with him.

For a while we walk in silence. Then Dad speaks. He says it's strange to think that he lived only a couple of miles away from here after he and my mum divorced. I've often thought the same when walking these ancient, meandering tracks; wondered even whether one might snake off through the fields to emerge by his old front door. And I've wondered too what I'd find if I took it. But when I ask if he ever came to this place back then he shakes his head. 'Nope,' he says. I understand why. The river at the bottom of the track is a thick arm thrown around the town's unruly urban edge. The wild margin between the two appears rough, unloved, inglorious; appears, that is, until you wander into it. Then it turns into something else. An extraordinary place, unchanging – and ever-changing.

Along the holloway are further signs that winter is leaching from the land. Primroses bloom on the banks. Rabbits have thrown up soil for new burrows; it spills ochre-red over a collapsed wall and lacy trails of ivy, goose grass and miniature nettles. Crab apples and hazels explode with blackbirds. Males jump about in front of each other like fencers looking for a first strike. Dad stops by a gap in the screen of trees to raise his camera and take a view of the open field and pylons beyond. But my eyes automatically search the ground, for it was exactly here a few weeks ago that I found – and lost – the ring.

I'd been walking at dusk when, through the same hole beside the oak, I glimpsed a roe deer creeping along the far side of the field. Kneeling on the newly ploughed soil, I watched it feed, ears twitching, until it slipped soundlessly into the wood. Then, as I braced to push myself up, I felt something under my hand: a piece of metal on the edge of a clod of turned earth. Free of dirt it looked like an old ring, damaged by plough blade, flattened and dull. There was no jewel or intricacy, just what – in the half-light – passed for two clasped hands rendered crudely in the metal. I jumped up excitedly and, as I did, hit my head on a low branch, causing me to drop the ring back into the black soil. And despite searching until it was dark, I couldn't find it.

Standing here again, I think of how it came to be lost. I imagine a labourer at harvest time, red and dust-flecked, pushing it on to his sweetheart's finger as they sit looking westward, drinking the weak beer she's brought him in a stoneware jar. Perhaps the ring was always too large and, years later, it slipped from her sweaty knuckle as she helped load sheaves of wheat into a cart. Perhaps it was thrown at him in disgust. Or perhaps as an old man he buried it here as an act of remembrance – marking the place where long ago a promise was made.

I look up. Above the fields now the sky is still pale but lightening. Rooks *yak-yak* from the wood. Dad is still lining up the photograph: 'I can't really capture it,' he says. I push through the gap to join him, clear my throat and find my voice. 'Dad. I want to tell you something.'

As they leave my mouth, the words send a ripple of emotion through my body, a wave that I watch wash from me to my father. And I see his face crack and shift from surprise and concern to grinning; his eyes widen with delight and shock. 'But that's fantastic news,' he laughs. '*Fantastic!*'

His reaction is so sudden and instinctive that it makes me well up. 'You can't tell anyone yet,' I say. 'It's too early.'

'No, no, of course.'

'Promise?'

'I promise.'

The rest of the walk is a confusing blur of outside and inside worlds. Whatever we look at or start talking about, the conversation soon slips back to the baby. Dad stops intermittently, smiles and exclaims things like: 'It *is* wonderful. Really. I'm delighted.' Never does he mention money or jobs; instead he tells me how I'll be a great father and that I should spend as much time I can with the baby when it comes. 'I worked too hard sometimes when you and your brother were small,' he says. 'I wish now I could have been out here more, in places like this, with you both. Maybe I got the ratio wrong.' I've never heard him say anything like this before. I feel a strange sense of openness and I tease him that he can babysit any time he wants. 'I will,' he says. 'I want to.'

It's not until we're back at the start that I realise how liberating it feels that he should be so enlivened by this secret he's carrying. There is fresh blood in his bones. And while I wait for him to change his shoes, I take in the hawthorn growing over the sidings, the opening buds and the foxglove leaves. The trees on either side of the old railway are alive with song and made even more beautiful by the way their highest, thinnest twigs amass in vein-like clusters, lit by an egg-yolk sun. They look like bees' wings, poised and primed for flight, trembling in the soft breeze. Everything is brimming with possibility. Everything is pointing forward to what is to come. And isn't that the way with spring? It feels sweeter even than the highest summer day because it arrives while winter still holds the earth. Like the birdsong washing over Britain in the pre-dawn, spring emerges from the dark.

Rob Cowen, 2016

A Backward Spring

The trees are afraid to put forth buds,
And there is timidity in the grass;
The plots lie gray where gouged by spuds,
And whether next week will pass
Free of sly sour winds is the fret of each bush
Of barberry waiting to bloom.

Yet the snowdrop's face betrays no gloom,
And the primrose pants in its heedless push,
Though the myrtle asks if it's worth the fight
This year with frost and rime
To venture one more time
On delicate leaves and buttons of white
From the selfsame bough as at last year's prime,
And never to ruminate on or remember
What happened to it in mid-December.

Thomas Hardy, 1917

March, and the sap is rising. Sparrows fly past the window bearing nesting materials, and the woods that lie a short stroll from home are luring me once more. Eythorne, this small Kent village, is not so different from many others, perhaps distinctive solely for the countryside that surrounds it. I stand looking at the pockets of woodland from the bathroom window as I brush my teeth. I could be there in ten minutes, I'd like to be there at once, but I have to get dressed. It's not that we stopped walking that way through the colder months, only now there's a new urge to step out and witness all the rapid changes, to see what's being proclaimed from small yet confident beaks across the gardens and down the lanes. Just days ago a light frost covered the lawn and wood smoke billowed from chimneys here, a scene held in a pale watercolour wash of winter. Soon my seven-year-old sees me pulling on my boots and grabs her pink binoculars. It's 6.30 a.m., and the sun is out. I scribble a note for the rest of the family – *Gone to the woods* – I know they'll understand.

Gaudy daffodils of poster-paint yellow shine from front gardens like Easter craft daubed by small hands. On the house that marks the entrance to the woods jackdaws are nesting in an old Victorian chimney pot. One stands sentinel as its partner comes and goes.

From the woodland path we can hear great spotted woodpeckers drumming the trees, their way of finding a mate and marking territory in the absence of an adequate song. The pecking comes at different pitches and I wonder if this is in part due to the thickness of a particular tree trunk, to differing degrees of hollowness. The sound leads us on like the Pied Piper, with one beat seeming to come from inside the tallest beech tree at the badger sett. We stop beneath it and the bird is quiet. My daughter uses her binoculars, but I'm more focused on inspecting the holes around and about, the badgers' welfare being the main reason that I come to the woods throughout the year. All is well here, they are being left alone for now, though the cull in other parts of the country has been taken by some as a green light to interfere.

My local badgers have been dragging out their bedding to air for a number of weeks, a sure sign they've been nesting. Cubs are usually born between January and March, and most will be getting used to their network of tunnels, perhaps approaching the exit holes to investigate the intriguing sounds and smells that reach them from outside.

We continue our circuit, which takes us along the field edge, and spot a Brimstone butterfly dancing over the crop of barley, our first this year. They are known to be a marker of spring, their emergence from hibernation a signal that the seasons are turning. Soon they will blend in with the barley as it ripens, but for now they are easy to follow. A pair of chaffinches fly in unison, rising and falling together like dolphins before diving into the wood. Out across the field a kestrel is soaring, enjoying the sun on its wings while we admire its pink-brown markings from below.

The path leads us into the woods again, and here the birdsong is intense. With them all singing together it is hard to pick out one voice, the all-familiar robins, blackbirds and pigeons now mixed in a chorus of sound. The simplicity of their song throughout the winter has helped the children learn some of the native species, but I had forgotten what a joyful crescendo this season brings.

Across the woodland floor anemones are opening up, tentatively unfurling as they begin to trust the show of early warmth. The canopy of beech in this small spinney has yet to reappear and block out their light.

Back home the family will be getting up and we haven't eaten breakfast, so we head for the village. I'm reassured that the woodland is waking from its winter slumber, but if I'm honest it's the badgers I really want to see.

Soon the month turns into April and Easter Sunday brings a day of sustained sunshine. Days like this usually encourage the badgers out early and by 7.30 in the evening I'm walking into the woods again with my husband and thirteen-year-old daughter. It's our first attempt at badger-watching this year, aside from the night footage caught on my Nature Cam when we're fast asleep in bed.

There is a spiritual feel to the wood tonight that I don't think I'm imagining. Perhaps it's expectation, and awe that this recently denuded scene is now bursting into life again. The winds have stopped and our sense of anticipation seems to be shared by nature, waiting with us. A blackbird shrieks an alarm call in front of us, as if to dispel such romantic notions. Then a young rabbit hops down the badger hole that we're looking at. I wonder if it's disused now – though the sett is still active the badgers may adopt other holes as their main entrances and exits. I can hear a faint mewing noise coming from underfoot; it's not impossible that we may hear the badgers below ground, and wild animals are no more able to keep their children quiet than we are. Our youngest is keen to start badger-watching this spring, but I'm not sure she'll be able to stop talking for long enough.

My daughter is nudging me. 'Look!' she hisses. '*Badgers.*' I just catch a glimpse of an adult walking behind a tree twenty metres away, but it's enough to savour for a while. The evening is getting colder; though I'm wearing gloves the winter chill is still to be felt, throbbing in my thumb with the intensity of a deep cut. But it's worth it. Before long we are all experiencing it and catch each others' eyes.

'One cub was tiny. Its head was the size of a jacket potato – like this,' says Maddy as we turn to leave, stretching out her hand. I believe her – and I'm always relieved when the children have had sightings. I'm just happy to be out here, and badger moments are an added bonus. And there will always be next time.

Caroline Greville, 2016

The Mole had been working very hard all the morning, spring-cleaning his little home. First with brooms, then with dusters; then on ladders and steps and chairs, with a brush and a pail of whitewash; till he had dust in his throat and eyes, and splashes of whitewash all over his black fur, and an aching back and weary arms. Spring was moving in the air above and in the earth below and around him, penetrating even his dark and lowly little house with its spirit of divine discontent and longing. It was small wonder, then, that he suddenly flung down his brush on the floor, said 'Bother!' and 'O blow!' and also 'Hang spring-cleaning!' and bolted out of the house without even waiting to put on his coat. Something up above was calling him imperiously, and he made for the steep little tunnel which answered in his case to the gavelled carriage-drive owned by animals whose residences are nearer to the sun and air. So he scraped and scratched and scrabbled and scrooged and then he scrooged again and scrabbled and scratched and scraped, working busily with his little paws and muttering to himself, 'Up we go! Up we go!' till at last, pop! his snout came out into the sunlight, and he found himself rolling in the warm grass of a great meadow.

'This is fine!' he said to himself. 'This is better than white-washing!' The sunshine struck hot on his fur, soft breezes caressed his heated brow, and after the seclusion of the cellarage he had lived in so long the carol of happy birds fell on his dulled hearing almost like a shout. Jumping off all his four legs at once, in the joy of living and the delight of spring without its cleaning, he pursued his way across the meadow till he reached the hedge on the further side.

'Hold up!' said an elderly rabbit at the gap. 'Sixpence for the privilege of passing by the private road!' He was bowled over in an instant by the impatient and contemptuous Mole, who trotted along the side of the hedge chaffing the other rabbits as they peeped hurriedly from their holes to see what the row was about. 'Onion-sauce! Onion-sauce!' he remarked jeeringly, and was gone before they could think of a thoroughly satisfactory reply. Then they all started grumbling at each other. 'How STUPID you are! Why didn't you tell him——' 'Well, why didn't YOU say——' 'You might have reminded him——' and so on, in the usual way; but, of course, it was then much too late, as is always the case.

It all seemed too good to be true. Hither and thither through the meadows he rambled busily, along the hedgerows, across the copses, finding everywhere birds building, flowers budding, leaves thrusting – everything happy, and progressive, and occupied. And instead of having an uneasy conscience pricking him and whispering 'whitewash!' he somehow could only feel how jolly it was to be the only idle dog among all these busy citizens. After all, the best part of a holiday is perhaps not so much to be resting yourself, as to see all the other fellows busy working.

He thought his happiness was complete when, as he meandered aimlessly along, suddenly he stood by the edge of a full-fed river. Never in his life had he seen a river before – this sleek, sinuous, full-bodied animal, chasing and chuckling, gripping things with a gurgle and leaving them with a laugh, to fling itself on fresh playmates that shook themselves free, and were caught and held again. All was a-shake and a-shiver – glints and gleams and sparkles, rustle and swirl, chatter and bubble. The Mole was bewitched, entranced, fascinated. By the side of the river he trotted as one trots, when very small, by the side of a man who holds one spell-bound by exciting stories; and when tired at last, he sat on the bank, while the river still chattered on to him, a babbling procession of the best stories in the world, sent from the heart of the earth to be told at last to the insatiable sea.

As he sat on the grass and looked across the river, a dark hole in the bank opposite, just above the water's edge, caught his eye, and dreamily he fell to considering what a nice snug dwelling-place it would make for an animal with few wants and fond of a bijou riverside residence, above flood level and remote from noise and dust. As he gazed, something bright and small seemed to twinkle down in the heart of it, vanished, then twinkled once more like a tiny star. But it could hardly be a star in such an unlikely situation; and it was too glittering and small for a glow-worm. Then, as he looked, it winked at him, and so declared itself to be an eye; and a small face began gradually to grow up round it, like a frame round a picture.

A brown little face, with whiskers.

A grave round face, with the same twinkle in its eye that had first attracted his notice.

Small neat ears and thick silky hair.

It was the Water Rat!

Kenneth Grahame, The Wind in the Willows, *1908*

Butterflies, when they appear early, are some times forerunners of fine weather. The first sort which appears in spring is the sulphur butterfly *Papilio sulphurea proecox,* whose wings are of pale greenish yellow. These come in March if the weather be fine and warm. The next sort are the tortoiseshell butterflies, early in April. And in May come the common white or cabbage butterflies. Moths and Sphinxes are also signs of fine weather, when they are common in an evening.

Thomas Furly Forster, The Pocket Encyclopaedia of Natural Phenomena, *published 1827*

Spring arrives differently in the night garden. Much of the action happens while humans are tucked up inside with the curtains drawn shut against the chilly dark. But around the time frogs spawn – or perhaps a little earlier if we've had a balmy spell – the hedgehogs wake up.

'I remember hedgehogs,' people say. 'You used to see them all the time, but not now. There are none left round our way.' It's true that the population's suffered a dramatic decline, from 36 million in the 1950s to less than one million today. And yet for all that there are still tens of thousands of us who share our lives with hedgehogs. We just don't always realise it.

Because hedgehogs are nocturnal, they're easy to overlook. They're unassuming animals, not given to draw attention to themselves unless caught up in the throes of grunty sex. When the crocuses shrivel and flop like deflated balloons and the forsythia comes into bloom, I go searching for scat on the lawn. Hog poo consists of small, neat, inoffensive chipolatas that are black or dark brown and often glittery with beetle remains. You'll find them deposited in the borders or tucked away against the hedge. As soon as I spot the first one, I set up my Bushnell trail cam and break out the peanuts. Monitoring can begin.

'We have a hedgehog who visits,' a girlfriend told me. Does she – or does she in fact have several? Variations in size apart, it's very difficult to tell one individual from another. The only reason I realised I had multiple hogs was because I happened to catch them on film together. Four at once has been my record.

But if they come separately, how are you supposed to count them? I did some research and found out the British Hedgehog Preservation Society endorses careful marking of hogs for recording purposes. Humbrol enamel paint is what the BHPS recommend, the sort you buy in a model shop, applied with a small brush and extreme caution to the tips of the spines only. I chose Brilliant White because I knew it would show up on film.

The first few times I marked a hog I did it on the lawn while the animal carried on feeding. If you approach cautiously and with due respect you can easily get within touching distance, as hedgehogs are of a phlegmatic disposition. However, as my confidence grew, I began to pick them up and bring them inside for a once-over. They never minded as long as I was quick. Ecologist Hugh Warwick, author of *A Prickly Affair*, taught me how to sex a hog: boars have what looks like an 'outie' tummy button, and sows don't. I would also pop the animal on the kitchen scales to record its weight, and check for ticks and flesh wounds. Oven gloves are useful here.

Once you can identify specific hogs, then reviewing a spring evening's footage becomes like watching a soap opera. Familiar characters display particular traits, and a pecking order becomes clear. For instance *L*, a hog I was asked to foster by a rescue centre, turned out to be a massive bully. He'd been shy and compliant whilst I was feeding him up in the shed. Once released, though, he'd charge onto the scene so aggressively that the other hogs would curl in fear. He'd then take a run and bowl them away, one after another, into the flowerbeds. Only when his field was clear would he go back and eat.

Y-Boy's single mission in life, on the other hand, was to mate. He couldn't have cared less what the rest of the boars were up to. Most evenings he was to be found circling a sow and huffing at her, a performance that could last up to an hour. Several times he got as far as climbing on top, only for her to walk off, distracted. Some nights even he himself would pause for a snack. What an effort it all looked. No one seemed to be having much fun. It made me wonder how baby hedgehogs ever get conceived.

Spring's become the time of year I walk down the street and neighbours call out to me, 'I see your hedgehogs are out of hibernation! I had one in the back last night.' 'Rainbow' lives across the road behind a broken wall-grating. 'Smallbum' moved all the way up to the corner, twelve houses away, and settled there. 'Diagonal' comes from somewhere across the back lane. All humans in the road have been leafleted with a Hedgehog Wish-list (dish of water, meaty cat food or mealworms, holes in the fence) and Potential Hazards (ground netting, uncovered drains, slippery-sided ponds, strimmers). We're becoming the kind of joined-up-garden community where hedgehogs really thrive.

After dark, though, it's just me and my little patch. The night world wakes up and it's a world independent of me, secretive and urgent. Early moths take wing in the cold air while wood mice hop through the tree roots. Frogs gather, and newts kiss the surface of the pond. Somewhere above me is a small bat. And now the hedgehogs come. Here they are, trundling down the lawn on their cabriole legs, to tell me we're off! We're up and running, the year's begun again and we all have our business to attend to.

I turn on the camera, and go inside.

Kate Long, 2016

It is sweet on awaking in the early morn to listen to the small bird singing on the tree. No sound of voice or flute is like to the bird's song; there is something in it distinct and separate from all other notes. The throat of woman gives forth a more perfect music, and the organ is the glory of man's soul. The bird upon the tree utters the meaning of the wind – a voice of the grass and wild flower, words of the green leaf; they speak through that slender tone. Sweetness of dew and rifts of sunshine, the dark hawthorn touched with breadths of open bud, the odour of the air, the colour of the daffodil – all that is delicious and beloved of spring-time are expressed in his song. Genius is nature, and his lay, like the sap in the bough from which he sings, rises without thought. Nor is it necessary that it should be a song; a few short notes in the sharp spring morning are sufficient to stir the heart. But yesterday the least of them all came to a bough by my window, and in his call I heard the sweet-briar wind rushing over the young grass. Refulgent fall the golden rays of the sun; a minute only, the clouds cover him and the hedge is dark. The bloom of the gorse is shut like a book; but it is there – a few hours of warmth and the covers will fall open. The meadow is bare, but in a little while the heart-shaped celandine leaves will come in their accustomed place. On the pollard willows the long wands are yellow-ruddy in the passing gleam of sunshine, the first colour of spring appears in their bark. The delicious wind rushes among them and they bow and rise; it touches the top of the dark pine that looks in the sun the same now as in summer; it lifts and swings the arching trail of bramble; it dries and crumbles the earth in its fingers; the hedge-sparrow's feathers are fluttered as he sings on the bush.

I wonder to myself how they can all get on without me – how they manage, bird and flower, without me to keep the calendar for them. For I noted it so carefully and lovingly, day by day, the seed-leaves on the mounds in the sheltered places that come so early, the pushing up of the young grass, the succulent dandelion, the coltsfoot on the heavy, thick clods, the trodden chickweed despised at the foot of the gate-post, so common and small, and yet so dear to me. Every blade of grass was mine, as though I had planted it separately. They were all my pets, as the roses the lover of his garden tends so faithfully. All the grasses of the meadow were my pets, I loved them all; and perhaps that was why I never had a 'pet,' never cultivated a flower, never kept a caged bird, or any creature. Why keep pets when every wild free hawk that passed overhead in the air was mine? I joyed in his swift, careless flight, in the throw of his pinions, in his rush over the elms and miles of woodland; it was happiness to see his unchecked life. What more beautiful than the sweep and curve of his going through the azure sky? These were my pets, and all the grass. Under the wind it seemed to dry and become grey, and the starlings running to and fro on the surface that did not sink now stood high above it and were larger. The dust that drifted along blessed it and it grew. Day by day a change; always a note to make. The moss drying on the tree trunks, dog's-mercury stirring under the ash-poles, bird's-claw buds of beech lengthening; books upon books to be filled with these things. I cannot think how they manage without me.

To-day through the window-pane I see a lark high up

against the grey cloud, and hear his song. I cannot walk about and arrange with the buds and gorse-bloom; how does he know it is the time for him to sing? Without my book and pencil and observing eye, how does he understand that the hour has come? To sing high in the air, to chase his mate over the low stone wall of the ploughed field, to battle with his high-crested rival, to balance himself on his trembling wings outspread a few yards above the earth, and utter that sweet little loving kiss, as it were, of song – oh, happy, happy days! So beautiful to watch as if he were my own, and I felt it all! It is years since I went out amongst them in the old fields, and saw them in the green corn; they must be dead, dear little things, by now. Without me to tell him, how does this lark to-day that I hear through the window know it is his hour?

The green hawthorn buds prophesy on the hedge; the reed pushes up in the moist earth like a spear thrust through a shield; the eggs of the starling are laid in the knot-hole of the pollard elm – common eggs, but within each a speck that is not to be found in the cut diamond of two hundred carats – the dot of protoplasm, the atom of life. There was one row of pollards where they always began laying first. With a big stick in his beak the rook is blown aside like a loose feather in the wind; he knows his building-time from the fathers of his house – hereditary knowledge handed down in settled course: but the stray things of the hedge, how do they know? The great blackbird has planted his nest by the ash-stole, open to every one's view, without a bough to conceal it and not a leaf on the ash – nothing but the moss on the lower end of the branches. He does not seek cunningly for concealment. I think of the drift of time, and I see the apple bloom coming and the blue veronica in the grass. A thousand thousand buds and leaves and flowers and blades of grass, things to note day by day, increasing so rapidly that no pencil can put them down and no book hold them, not even to number them – and how to write the thoughts they give? All these without me – how can they manage without me?

For they were so much to me, I had come to feel that I was as much in return to them. The old, old error: I love the earth, therefore the earth loves me – I am her child – I am Man, the favoured of all creatures. I am the centre, and all for me was made.

Richard Jefferies, 'Hours of Spring', Field and Hedgerow; Being the Last Essays of Richard Jefferies, *1889*

I have come to the loch today to write my journal precisely because it is such an uplifting morning. I don't normally. My routine is to take rough notes as it pleases me and return to my desk after a walk and write it up at some idle moment of the day when pressing things are done. But after the long winter there are forces inside desperate to get out when the day is seductive and anodyne like today. Winter walks have been fine – good, bracing, ear-tingling sorties, often more to do with gloves and scarves and steaming breath than with observation of wildlife and any focused attempt to feel at one with the natural world. Back then the feel-good factor came afterwards, a 'well-I-did-it' glow of achievement only experienced when I was back at the fireside, quite different from this 'what-a-hell-of-a-place-to-sit-and-work' sensation that's overwhelming me today.

There are other reasons for being here right now. Some years the Highland spring can last for only a few days. May is still capable of snow showers, although they won't stay – 'lambing storms', my crofter neighbours call them, with that terse and comprehending cynicism that so often defines their byre and baler-twine brand of wisdom, garnered over centuries of hard-won pragmatism – sending everything scurrying for cover again for as long as they last. And then June can suddenly soar to lofty temperatures on static anti-cyclonic highs that dawdle through long days of mackerel-feathered, cirro-stratus blue. Searing through thin, dry air the UV is merciless, bringing a first ruddy blush to the pallid cheeks of winter. Before we know it, summer is firing in.

These bug-free early days must be grabbed. The Highland midge, that scourge of humid days to come, is as yet still a maggoty little larva hiding in its millions in the peaty ooze of the marsh. But the earth is absorbent, the warmth of the sun is piercing and probing deep into the soil and the damp, winter-killed vegetation. The great reawakening, silent and invisible, is mustering its armies twenty-four hours a day. Soon the insect harvest will erupt in all its rampant, multifarious forms, from the exquisitely refined, like the first speckled wood butterflies that any day now will delicately lift from the path beneath my feet, to the execrable great diving beetle, the scourge of the loch's edge, whose calliper-mandibled larva lurks among the rotting stems of last year's water lilies, waiting for what must be its high point of the season. When the toad and frog tadpoles fatten and wiggle free from their natal plasma, this dragon of the murky shallows embarks upon a feeding frenzy, seizing tadpole after tadpole in ferocious, hypodermic jaws, injecting them with a cocktail of pernicious digestive acids which, in the space of a few minutes, without ever letting go, dissolve the tadpoles' insides to a protein soup so that the larva can suck them dry.

From the peaty sludge in the loch's deeps, from the soggy sedge blanket of the marsh, in the root-caves of trees, beneath the rufous bark flakes of pines, deep within dead logs and decaying fence posts, snug inside soft moss cushions and the surface inches of the soil, under rocks and stones, a horde of creeping, flying, crawling and slithering wildlife is fingering the solar pulse. Armoured legs are creaking, suckers are opening and closing, wing veins are pumping up, jaws are hungrily flexing and twitching antennae are tentatively reaching out, probing the possibilities of the future.

These are precious days of warmth and excitement, days a naturalist cannot afford to miss. If I have to go away I can't wait to get home again, hurrying up the loch path to check out the incalculable, unsleeping and effervescent metamorphosis of spring. Dawns cry out for attendance, dusks are just as alluring. I struggle to know which to exploit, often giving in to both. To sit quietly beside the loch at either end of these rapturous spring days delivers a soul-exalting equanimity I have never achieved anywhere else in the world.

Sir John Lister-Kaye, At the Water's Edge: A Walk in the Wild, *2010*

Spring. A time of transformation. It is now that skeins of wild geese and winter wigeon yield the skies to a myriad springtime migrants, for many people the most conspicuous sign of the changing season. Countless nature lovers wait for the first swallow, cuckoo or lark. But, lost and ignored amid the brighter, more alluring swifts, sedge warblers and sandwich terns, one of my favourite songbirds makes its triumphant return to our shores: the chiffchaff, a bird that embodies the very spirit of spring.

For me, spring commences with the first chiffchaff and its first song, often voiced from high in the canopy, the bird obscured behind a veil of fresh green leaves. The chiffchaff does not showcase the lyrical genius of the nightingale, nor does it boast the imitative skill of the marsh warbler. But the repetitive '*chiff-chaff, chiff-chaff*' evokes bursting buds, frogspawn, daffodils, lengthier days and warmer nights. It's a characteristic and charming tune interrupted only by a sporadic 'hweet' as the bird skips energetically from branch to branch.

Due to its broad habitat tolerance, the chiffchaff is often the first returning songster to be noted, arriving in late March before many other species. It is a versatile breeding bird. Unlike other spring migrants, such as the altitude-addicted ring ouzel or pernickety whinchat, the chiffchaff is unfussy and adaptive, happy with coastal thickets, conifer plantations, parks, gardens, deciduous woodlands and mature hedgerows alike.

Distinguishable from its close cousin, the willow warbler, by its black legs and constant tail flicking, the chiffchaff's appearance is for many people not very inspiring. In fact, the humble chiff virtually embodies the term 'little brown job' or 'LBJ', a phrase thrown about by birders in relation to dull and lacklustre species. But from its glaring white supercilium to its fine, insect-snatching bill, the chiffchaff is a pleasure to behold if seen well. Its subtle shades complement the season perfectly. Young birds boast a palette of yellow and green on a par with the freshest hawthorn buds, while adults bear warmer tones reminiscent of last year's falling leaves.

A chiffchaff's nest is a beauty to behold if ever you get the chance. Provided you take care, a quick glance will not harm the bird. It is testament to the ingenuity of nature: a small, intricate dome of dead stems and leaves fashioned painstakingly by the female as her mate stands sentinel nearby, relentlessly defending the nest from adversaries large and small. Inside, a clutch of eggs, gleaming white and speckled with black, snuggle amid a thick layer of feathers collected by the hen. Somewhat plain eggs, dowdy-coloured, but perfect if viewed with an appreciation for simplicity. Rather like the chiffchaff itself. There truly is a lot more to this feisty, endearing bird than meets the eye. Where others might see a rather dull and vocally maladroit visitor, I see beauty and brilliance in equal measure, combined with unusual bravery for a bird no bigger than a blue tit. I encourage everyone to appreciate the chiffchaff for what it is: a seasonal sensation.

James Common, 2016

The Voice of Spring

I come, I come! ye have called me long;
I come o'er the mountains, with light and song.
Ye may trace my step o'er the waking earth
By the winds which tell of the violet's birth,
By the primrose stars in the shadowy grass,
By the green leaves opening as I pass.

I have breathed on the South, and the chestnut-flowers
By thousands have burst from the forest bowers,
And the ancient graves and the fallen fanes
Are veiled with wreaths on Italian plains;
But it is not for me, in my hour of bloom,
To speak of the ruin or the tomb!

I have looked o'er the hills of the stormy North,
And the larch has hung all his tassels forth;
The fisher is out on the sunny sea,
And the reindeer bounds o'er the pastures free,
And the pine has a fringe of softer green,
And the moss looks bright, where my step has been.

I have sent through the wood-paths a glowing sigh,
And called out each voice of the deep blue sky,
From the night-bird's lay through the starry time,

SPRING

In the groves of the soft Hesperian clime,
To the swan's wild note by the Iceland lakes,
When the dark fir-branch into verdure breaks.

From the streams and founts I have loosed the chain;
They are sweeping on to the silvery main,
They are flashing down from the mountain brows,
They are flinging spray o'er the forest boughs,
They are bursting fresh from their sparry caves,
And the earth resounds with the joy of waves.

Felicia Hemans, 1823

Spring arrived at Cley Marshes this morning in the shape of a bird. So smart, with his grey head and back, black bandit cheek mask, black wings and warm yellow underparts; not a feather out of place. My first wheatear of the year, with a flash of his white rump, flits out of sight over the edge of Cley's shingle bank, leaving me wondering just how far this bird has travelled, and where he may be by tomorrow.

Cley springs are full of such miracles. Today the green jungle of alexanders plants edging the path to the reed-thatched hides has gained a voice. Hidden sedge warblers are in full song. One, unable to contain this surge of spring energy, flies up to hover, still singing, in full view over the boardwalk.

I got to Cley early today and, even before I saw them, I could hear the strange, wild music of lapwings in display: tumbling like crazy aerial acrobats, their power dives, stoops and climbs would put any human air-show to shame. It's one of my favourite spring spectacles and I haven't even reached the hides! Overhead a whimbrel calls, then a swallow skims the still winter-brown reeds. High above me are more swallows, and with them sand martins. As I walk towards the hides I can hear the 'klute' calls of avocets, the noisy peeps of oystercatchers and the whistles of redshanks. It's going to be a good morning.

The view from the reed-thatched hides is over shallow freshwater pools fringed by still winter-brown reeds. Dunlin are busy feeding at the water's edge, probing the mud, constantly moving, running, making short flights, wheeling in small, tight groups only to land again and feed with an urgency driven by the lengthening days. Spring is calling these birds north, and in a few days they will have left these pools on journeys I can scarcely imagine. Where will they be in a week's time? Some will head up our east coast, perhaps flying day and night to the still snow-covered tundras of Iceland. Some will stop there and breed, others continue to the east coast of Greenland where Arctic foxes and powerful-winged gyrfalcons are new dangers they must face.

There are challenges even today. Suddenly every bird that was feeding stops – it's as if just for a moment someone hit the pause button – then bedlam, and every bird is in flight. Waders are wheeling, lapwings rocketing skywards and birds I hadn't even noticed: teal from hidden shallows in the reeds, a snipe zig-zagging skywards and, dwarfing the dunlin, with long beaks and white wing bars, eight black-tailed godwits join the mêlée. One of Cley's breeding marsh harriers, a chocolate brown female with creamy crown and just a hint of cream on the leading edge of strong broad wings is powering low over the water. She follows the edge of the reeds. This is no gentle soaring on shallow 'V' shaped wings – everything about this bird says focus and intent and then, in just a moment, as quickly as she appeared, she's gone – and the dunlin and their migratory relatives are back to the serious business of feeding. Each returning group lands as 'birds of a feather'. Birds that were wheeling overhead in aerial chaos now sort themselves into tight, single-species flocks, dunlin, teal, godwit and lapwing each finding their own perfect niche. Several scaly-backed ruff have joined this spring feeding frenzy. If the weather stays bright and clear they may cross the North

Sea this evening on a single flight taking them to Denmark or Norway. Some will go further, perhaps to Russia, following, for at least part of their journey, not footsteps, but wing-beats, of birds like the thousands of Brent geese that left these marshlands at Cley in late February and early March.

But the spring morning is too perfect for spending long inside a hide, however impressive the spectacle. Sunshine and a southerly breeze make a walk down Cley's East Bank a delight. I'm lucky, as this is a regular walk for me, but in the last few months winter has been slow to release her grip and I have become used to fighting my way into the teeth of a northerly gale and dodging showers. Today, though, spring is finally here. Its voice is a skylark lost in a clear blue sky over the saltings of Arnold's Marsh, while below it, and much easier to spot, several redshanks are in noisy display flights. Their wings flick in shallow, rapid beats. Sometimes they hover, proclaiming their rights to samphire and sea purslane estates where they hope a powerful voice and exuberant song-flight will prove irresistible to a female. By the time these marshes turn purple with sea lavender with luck their fluff-ball chicks with absurdly long legs will be picking tiny insects from creek edges and salt marsh pools.

Today Arnold's Marsh is noisy with sandwich terns. With '*kirrick, kirrick*' calls and white wings that have borne them from the rich shallow waters of the West African coast, today they are settling back in for another busy breeding season. Males fly in off the sea. I only know these are males as each one bears a gift. A gift in glittering silver, a sand eel to present with much nodding and bowing and sky-pointing of beaks to the females lined up and waiting on the shingle edge of these saline lagoons. They won't stay here to breed but will move just a few kilometres west to the tip of Blakeney Point where they will be joined by several thousand others, making the largest breeding colony in Britain. Today, though, they are very much at home here at Cley. Are they pleased to be back? I like to think so.

David North, 2016

March Dust and May Sun, both of which imply a fine dry spring, are said to be particularly good omens for the husbandman. An adage says, 'A peck of March dust is worth a king's ransom.' We have confirmed, by many years' experience, the truth of the proverb which commends a dry spring, as leading to the most productive summer.

Thomas Furly Forster, The Pocket Encyclopaedia of Natural Phenomena, *published 1827*

At the southwesterly tip of Britain, amongst the low hills of Bodmin Moor, the river gathers in a furzey marsh. The waters move beneath the A30, pass through a drowned valley and muscle into miles of moorland fields. Further on, the water cuts through granite and bounces into pools cold enough for spawning salmon and sea trout.

The river sparkles past human dwellings: past drives, parked cars and gardens with swings and climbing frames where children play. The banks are knuckled with the roots of ash trees that otters use as covert passageways to hide from prying eyes. The fishy scent marks of their spraint linger on almost every prominent rock and could give them away to those who wish to pay attention. People who live beside the water might be in the know about their otter neighbours, but they could just as easily mistake the otter's comings and goings, and its characteristic whistle, for courting dippers or the chinking voices of nesting wrens.

The sprightly Fowey tumbles over rocks and through woodland, it races under bridges throwing moist spray that mists uncurling ferns on the banks. To save energy, otters come out of the water here and nose through the rich undergrowth where it is dry. Beneath the bridges aromatic masses of moss and fine, sandy silt build up. Here, the perfect wet surface captures the otters' movements in svelte trails, tracing evidence of their secret nightly commute.

A recently half-eaten duck might lie in the shallows. A fishbone. A small scrape of sand made by somebody with a heavy tail and a crescent of five webbed toes.

As the waters enter gentler slopes and the current slows, wild garlic and wood anemone carpet the banks. Tall, gnarly oaks are showing buds, and in the glades where the weak spring light comes through, patches of dog violet splash and scatter through the spindly hazel coppices. From the edge of distant villages, beyond the mosaic of reedy wetland and boggy fields, the voices of song thrushes speckle the air.

Where the first hint of an estuary begins, brackish creeks seep into the main river, and tributaries lined with copses of hazel and ash carry reflections of tight black buds. In its smooth sections the water absorbs all the brightness of filigree leaves just emerging. Where the light does not touch it, the water is musteline-black. In other stretches it turns to bottle glass, slow and green, with eel and bass swimming in its dreamy fathoms.

At dawn there is still a frail tissue of frost on the riverbank. Ice crystals carry a sliver of tracks that soon melt into the sand. A small female has passed, leaving an ottery shimmy behind. It is hard to say which way she might have gone, and her soft scent trail drains quickly away into the water. Through the overhanging hazel branches, shadows and light catch on catkins and reveal the bright red of bare dogwood twigs.

At the inter-tidal zone silty banks should make it easier to find otter tracks, but the tides can wash away any evidence. A little further seaward, salt marsh and mudflats spread into an oasis of sheeny openness. Wading birds, herons, water rail and moorhens might fall prey to the otters if they nest too close to the water. As the river's wildness becomes tamed and controlled by urban encroachment the sounds and scents of the human Riviera take over. Groynes, flood banks, roads; salt and vinegar, ketchup and beer; bottles litter the banks and smokers mingle with seaweed. The water might be watched from windows, walls, bridges and balconies, and the otters must slide past in the half-light, their profile sleeking into quieter nooks of the river where no trail can be seen.

There is something magical about the otter's continual sinking into a world where we cannot follow. Its disappearances have fascinated writers ever since we first wondered if we might try to capture it. Kenneth Grahame's childlike delight in this enigmatic side to lutrine behaviour is highlighted in Otter's abrupt vanishings in *The Wind in the Willows*. Otter often melts away unexpectedly in the midst of conversation, and consequently is thought to have no proper manners. Amongst the other animals it is accepted that this is simply how otters are, they vanish and nothing can be done about it. But the otter's riverine home also embodies an enticing mystery. For Henry Williamson, author of *Tarka the Otter*, the river could be a wraith-like creature, carrying memories of the land's history in its swirls and silvery mists. In *Tarka*, sibilant waters steal into the otter's holt and soothe him when he is afraid: wilder, fast moving stretches become creaturely at night, shiver to life and playfully tease and spar with Tarka, fighting him with watery teeth and star-streaming claws.

The indivisible nature of water and otters also appears in Charles Kingsley's childrens' story *The Water-Babies*. The water baby Tom sees a family of otters '. . . swimming about, and rolling, and diving, and twisting, and wrestling, and cuddling, and kissing and biting, and scratching, in the most charming fashion that ever was seen.'

In spring the river's bright weed fronds swirl like the hair of enchanted beings; rain-coloured herons stand like statues amongst the tips of new flag iris; pools of wriggling toadlets glisten, and mounds of emerald moss are magic enough. But the possibility of diving into this unreachable world rouses further with the promise of warm weather and soothing waves. Where the river meets the sea, gradations of blue deepen into the far horizon, and the sparkling indigo reminds me of the splashed seascapes painted by Kurt Jackson. Beyond the old granite quays and pale yellow sprigs of wild daffodils on the shore, I catch wildness in the call of an oystercatcher, the mew of a curlew and the high circling of gulls. Alongside it all, the otter sleeks in and out of the water, travelling upstream and down nightly, and most of us have no idea it is even there; we overlap but are only dimly aware of one another.

One evening, where the river pours into the estuary, I crawl dune-ward, crushing celandines in a curve of marsh scented by the tide's underbelly. Streetlight leaks from the town and drifts over the moving water so that any ripple or wavelet is thrown into sharp relief.

The otter's contact call can sound like the whistle of a kingfisher but when coupled with the heart-stopping sighting of a familiar, whiskered muzzle, there is no mistake. Tilting its head upward, it floats, crunches awkwardly through the hard shell of a small crab. I hear one faint call, catch the curve of its back as it disappears, and then nothing more. As the light fades I wonder at the lithe beauty of this creature. It must travel to the sea because it is hungry, starving perhaps, after the long winter. Here on the shore there must be more reliable feeding. My feet slick through the silty mud of the estuary: I need all my senses to find my way back to the solid world of pavement and road. Here where the season's edge blurs into another world, it's still possible to lose yourself in the wild.

Miriam Darlington, 2016

Quiet lies upon the fields and the woods this morning. No one is 'at plough', no one is carting. One might wonder what has happened but the familiar humming noise comes up from the rickyard, and skeins of black smoke are blurring the outlines of the leafless elms. Let us walk down to the farm, for surely this means that they are threshing.

As we come nearer, the humming noise is broken up into its parts; distinctly we hear the chug of the steam engine, the purr of the thresher and the clank of the elevator. These noises tell their tale of extreme activity long before we have turned the corner by the ash tree and can look down upon the rickyard.

It is a dull morning. The sky is monotonous grey; there is no wind to give shapes to clouds: and well it is so, for any breeze would blow the dust of the threshing into eyes and throats unbearably. Even as it is, everything is dimmed and blurred by the grain dust. The rickyard is enveloped in a golden fawny mist. The men's clothes may be blue, green or brown, but today they all look the same dust colour. The red of the threshing machine is muted by the dust. The men's beards are full of it; the blue of the elevator is no clearer.

And now, through this film one perceives the actors in the game, each in his place, like players in an orchestra. On top of the half-demolished grain stack five figures stand out dark against the sky, pitchforks at all angles as they pierce the sheaves of wheat that have lain packed there since last August, and throw them over to Ted Birkett, the 'feeder', who is huddled and squat inside the top of the thresher itself. Ted Birkett is over seventy and has been a 'drasher', as he calls it, his whole life. He travels about everywhere with the threshing machine as it moves with the steam engine and the engine man from farm to farm over the countryside; he is as much an attachment as if he were part of the machinery itself. With a rapid mechanical movement he cuts the binding straw of each sheaf as it is thrown to him, and liberates the wheat into the quivering, shaking maw of the thresher. He is a grumpy old man and has to be humoured by the entire threshing party. At the far end of the thresher, the machine throws out the straw, which rides up the elevator to the stack. Here pitchforks again seize it and spread it out flat on the ever-increasing straw stack.

All this time sacks are fastened to the thresher for the grain and rapidly these gaunt, flabby shapes fill and swell and solidify. Everything and everyone moves. Let any one figure cease for a moment and the link in the chain snaps. Nothing is still. The steam engine shakes as it belches out its black smoke, while its tight-flung belting moves round the cog of the thresher; the threshing machine incessantly quivers and throbs like a person in a state of great emotion, as it consumes and discharges its winnowed grain; men remove and weigh the full sacks and hoist them across shoulders and take them up tiny wooden steps to the granary, like figures in the background of a Dürer print.

A dog, chained to its kennel in the yard, wriggles unceasingly with excitement. Are there mice and rats tumbling down from the disturbed grain stack? On the stack itself is an agitated terrier, dodging the pitchforks of men as it rootles among the straw; the farmer's children are up there, too, with sticks, beating the stack to unearth the vermin. A mouse jumps over the edge of the stack and tumbles down the ladder. The dog in the kennel barks; the terrier whines. Life is surely worth living today, for man and dog and engine alike.

So this chain of labour runs on, hour after hour, grain stack shrinking in size, straw stack swelling, the elevator raised higher and higher.

On this March day dusk comes early, for the days are still short. The sky grows leaden in colour and the men on the ricks show up blurred against it. There is a flagging among the men. Dust has filled their noses and their throats; their muscles are tired. The grain stack is levelled to the ground. The straw stack towers above all else, loose and high. Jack is heard to grumble that he thinks he has done enough for one day.

'Seventy-four sacks and I've gone and carried, I have – seventy-four; and full, too, every one of them.'

Ted Birkett thinks it is time he knocked off work, too. It is he who insists on setting the pace. The engine is stopped; the smoke vanishes and gradually the chug of the engine and the purr of the thrasher grow slower and fainter, till the machines seem like large heavy animals falling asleep. Ted clambers doddering down the ladder, shaken by the diminishing tremors of the nodding thresher. His loose corduroy trousers flap as he climbs down, and he lands on the ground of the rickyard as the elevator chain gives its last heaving clank. In the sudden silence he shakes off the dust, and wipes his bowler hat with straw from the ground. It is a historic hat, worn by him each day for the past thirty years and cared for lovingly.

And now the rest of them slow down and stop. The ladder against the high straw stack trembles as the men step down it, pitchfork in hand. The top of the threshing machine is closed and a tarpaulin is spread over it. Soon everything is quiet, and the murmur of the men's voices grows fainter as they disperse to their homes for the night.

But the gleaners have ventured into the rickyard. Three farmyard cats, kings now of their own domain, slink around, hunting for mice that have managed to escape earlier in the day from the dogs; on the circular carpet of brushwood that is all that remains of the morning's grain stack, the farmyard fowls are busy, pecking at the wheat that has tumbled from the straw. What a scratching and fluttering there is in that small space.

Soon everything is quiet in the rickyard and even the hard shapes of the threshing machine and the engine grow softened and indistinct and withdraw into the dark of the night sky.

March is an unfriendly month, windy and rough and wet, with tantalising gleams of spring sunshine that encourage the little flowers in the coppice, only to let them be cruelly nipped by frosts. The fields are too wet for the plough and in this pause the farmer decides to thresh his remaining ricks. For several days now the air all around will be filled with the whirring, humming sound of the threshing machine. The ricks in the yard will have changed places as though a giant had been at play and had shifted them about. There is something eternal in this sound of threshing, even though it be made by machinery; it recalls the primeval songs of the women in the small islands of the Mediterranean as they chant in their strange Lydian mode to the horses and mules trotting round and round, blindfold, on a circle of sheaves, as they tread out the grain with their hoofs. For all sounds of the labours on the land date from the beginning of time.

Clare Leighton, The Farmer's Year: A Calendar of English Husbandry, *1933*

It is a cold Saturday in March. Winter's chill has returned with a biting wind and at the stream the bankside vegetation has been slow to start growing. So it is a joyful, totally unexpected and heart-warming surprise to see my first water vole of the year feeding on new celandine leaves. About fifteen feet away, it blends in with the bank so well that it is overlooked by most people crossing the bridge. It looks at me, having sensed that it has been spotted, as I begin to film it. Its blunt nose and charming, chubby face with hidden ears mark it out from a rat; but also, like all water voles, this one is very charismatic. It pauses for a moment before a dog barks and alarms it. Then it dives with a familiar plop and swims further downstream out of sight. The dive and 'plop!' is almost always a comical moment, and I walk back home on air.

Water voles are the UK's fastest declining mammal, so a sighting of one is always precious. Over the winter this one did not hibernate, but survived on protruding roots, and shoots it had stored in autumn in one of its burrow chambers. Each burrow complex will have nesting, food and latrine chambers with bolt holes positioned directly over water as a swift escape route. The male and female have separate chambers that they keep fastidiously tidy.

Water voles' contribution to a healthy wetland ecosystem is a vital one, increasing habitat diversity which in turn increases biodiversity. Having watched them for decades, I can immediately tell when a waterway is inhabited by voles as the plants will be species rich, lower in height due to their constant grazing, and looking healthy with little 'lawns' around their burrows. This grazing may even be deliberately done by breeding females as it leads to plenty of flowers and a pollen-rich source of protein for the period when they need to stay close to their young tucked away in the burrow.

Just two weeks later, towards the end of March, verdant spring vegetation has begun to grow. A quarter of a mile downstream I find a water vole tucking into one of its favourite plants: Fool's watercress. It is a veritable vegetable shredder and eats plants with amazing rapidity; no surprise, as they need to eat around 80 per cent of their body weight every day. Walking on, I find piles of their droppings, a sure sign that the breeding season has commenced. Females leave scent-marked droppings near their burrows to signal that they are in breeding condition; these are then counter-marked by males. A female will usually lay six latrines along her range. Their droppings are similar in shape and size to TicTacs and are usually blunt at both ends (unlike the rat whose droppings are larger and pointed at one end); colours vary depending upon what they've been eating. One autumn I found a pile of very red droppings, underneath a hawthorn bush laden with berries.

In spring, territorial disputes may occur between females competing for a male, who will have at least two breeding females in his range. One April I watched a fierce, if brief dispute that resulted in one female having her eye seriously damaged. When voles mate in water, it looks much like a minor squabble with lots of squeaking before the male rides on the female's back – though she will rebuff him fiercely if she is not ready. Just before her young are due to be born she will block the burrow entrance to protect them from predators; I usually see them around twenty-one days later, fluffy little chestnut-brown young chasing and play-fighting with each other while making high-pitched squeaks.

Water voles are close to the bottom of the food chain and are taken by otters, foxes, herons, owls, grass snakes, pike, stoats, weasels, cats and American Mink. Mink have been blamed for the sharp decline in water voles; a breeding female mink can eradicate a water vole colony in one breeding season. Foxes, though, could be the key to helping water voles to survive. They are out-competing non-native mink for prey, and when foxes are culled, research has shown that mink move back in.

On the last weekend in May I decide to visit Letcombe Brook, a much-loved childhood haunt. Here I saw my first water vole, sitting among water crowsfoot amid sparkling waters. Spring is in full swing, the voles have now had their first litter of the year, chiffchaffs and willow warblers are in full song and growth is burgeoning. The habitat along this crystal clear chalk stream looks ideal; a few steps more and there sits a vole in a hollow, almost hidden beneath thistle leaves. The bankside growth is now so lush and verdant that it is becoming difficult to spot them, so to see this one on the cusp of Summer is a joy. My first sighting was on a beautiful spring morning just like this one, and immediately I am a young, wide-eyed child again, looking with wonder at this delightful, charismatic animal. It is how my lifelong passion for water voles began; long may they live on our waterways and brighten our lives.

Jo Cartmell, 2016

And coming almost hand in hand with this catkin season there is another lovely aspect of spring, the phase of unopened buds. It is obscured again and again by the glories of crocus and primrose and daffodil, and if the weather is mild by the first blossoms of the flowering trees, which outshine it completely. The pink grace of the early almonds is not only lovely but easy to see. But the ruby buds of the birches are dark and obscure even in the March sunlight. The flowers of pyrus japonica on the south walls of houses open wide and flame crimson with all the delicacy and purity of single roses. But the golden buds of willows are golden only in sudden and accidental angles of light or against backgrounds of stormy cloud. They shine even then with a gold that has no counterpart in the colours of flowers, but with the soft and sombre light of polished wood, as though the buds were shining splinters of golden walnut.

The phase, always brief, represents in a sense a prologue to spring and at the same time an epilogue to winter, belonging all the time to neither one nor the other. The buds are awake but not open; they are no longer dead but still not alive. They have lost the colourlessness of winter, but there is no greenness in them. They are part of a kind of vernal twilight, a between season, a little interlude between one large act and another, an interlude that is all over and obscured and forgotten by the time the cuckoo is calling in the flowering ash trees.

Yet while it lasts, and however the weather may turn and change, from snow to sunlight or frost to rain, it seems to me to hold as much of the heart of spring as the almond and the daffodil. The south-west rain may smash and tear the crocuses like so many inside-out umbrellas to a ruin of gold and purple and white, but the rain profits the dark copses of birch and hazel and sweet chestnut so that they take on fresh beauty and life. The trees are liquid with colour. They stand drenched in wine-red or mauve or olive rain, the buds colouring the drops and the rain in turn richening the colour of the buds, so that the whole woodside gleams with the liquid passionate glow of multitudinous rain-drenched branches. And if the sun breaks out the rain against the buds is like still silver, or like blown beads of silver if the wind springs up. Whatever happens the buds, washed and slightly more rounded and swollen by the fresh rain, become glorified. Unlike the crocus or the daffodils or even the almonds, neither rain nor wind nor frost desolates them. They are fragile but strong. The buds of beech are like slender varnished chrysalises lying in light but secure sleep along the grey twigs. The buds of oak are like fat hard knobs of leather. The first buds of elm are little fluffy French knots of dark pink wool securely sewn on the jagged branches. The grey-black buds of the ash are like arrow heads of iron. They all have the common virtues of strength and delicacy. They all share a kind of delicate and subdued beauty. Individually they are no more than charming miniature shapes in dim pink or olive or mauve or grey or sepia. But collectively, in still or sunlit or wind-tossed multitudes, they transform the tree itself into a single colossal swaying and shining bud, an immense burning emblem of spring half-wakened.

And if this is very true of the larger trees and of the trees that grow naturally in great groups of one or many kinds, oaks and elms and beeches and sweet chestnut and birches, it is perhaps even truer of the lesser and rarer trees, sycamores and willows and alders and wild-cherries and beams and maples, whose buds have also the virtue of a greater individual loveliness. The buds of the sycamore are full silk shapes of creamy pink when young; there is something sweet and milky and virginal about them. And the maple buds, though so very like them, are smaller and less pink and silky. The wild cherry buds are gathered in little knots like brown beans at the tip of the smooth satin stems and on the hedges the buds of hawthorn and blackthorn, earliest to break, are like little beads of wine and cream. And in gardens and orchards the buds of peach and apple and pear are like taut nipples of pink-dove colour and white, full of the milk of the coming flower.

And loveliest of all, the young alder. Cut down, the alder shoots up again, like the sallow and the ash and the sweet-chesnut, with new long wands of sombre purple. The wood is too young to flower, but the leafbuds themselves have the shapely loveliness and enchantment of flowers just breaking, unfurling out of the bare stem like petals of smoky mauve, a strange rare colour, un-brilliant but rich, quiet but burning, that resembles the colour of sun-faded violets. There is a kind of bloom over the buds of the young alder, a soft cloudiness, which no other tree-buds ever seem to possess, but which is something peculiar to flowers of mauve and purple and lilac. There is the same mistiness of lovely bloom on the petals of summer irises, on the silky silver cups of pasque flowers, on clematis and campanulas and mauve geraniums and the dark unopened buds of lilac itself. It is the bloom of the plum and the grape and the wild sloe. There is something autumnal about it. So that the buds of the alder, so dark and soft and rich, seem to belong to another world, to be almost out of place among the pale colours and half-colours and gentle light and nakedness of first spring. They burn with the smoky darkness of some autumn fire.

And at the beginning of March, at the height of their beauty, it is suddenly as though their lilac smoke is spirited through all the wood and copses. The million buds of birch and hazel and chestnut and oak are suddenly on fire. The smoke is dark and still under cloud and rain, and then tawny in the sunlight and then still tawnier and richer and warmer as the days go past, until finally the sunlight starts it into an immense gold and emerald flame that spreads and intensifies until every bud on every tree is a green candle against the April sky.

And as the flame burns more fiercely and wonderfully the buds are consumed. The polished brown husks of the beeches fall down like ashes on the copper lawn of dead husks and leaves. The elm drops warm soft showers of fluffy fire. Ash and oak break into a flowering of mahogany and yellow, the wild cherry stands transfigured in white. The willows are turned to balloons of emerald, the horse-chestnut is glorious with pale brown flower-buds like those of Victorian wool, and Zaccheus could hide again in the sycamore. And the alder, once so splendid with purple fire, stands utterly insignificant, the purple gone, the tawny catkins withered, a little dark widow of a tree along the watersides, and buds everywhere are gone and forgotten as though they had never been.

H. E. Bates, Through the Woods: The English Woodland – April to April, *1936*

That's an interesting sight. A crow-like bird with a long tail carried a big twig in its beak. Its head and back, coloured black; belly white and the wings a deep blue. I didn't know its name, so I asked the woman nearby; she said it was a magpie. I felt a little stupid for asking, because I had seen the bird enough times. The bird jumped onto the platform, then down to the tracks. Why didn't it just fly? Then I realised that the twig was too heavy.

The bird carried the twig across the tracks with its chest out. It hurried as a train approached and jumped onto the other platform as it rushed past. A cool blast of wind followed behind the train but it wasn't as cold as the previous week. There had been a change; I felt it on my face, a little warmer and not so harsh.

The bird continued with its struggle, paused near the bottom of a wooden fence, then, with an effort, flew to the top. It perched, looking around, before flying high into the tree where it was making its nest.

Sunshine fell over the station. Mist evaporated off the fence, and everywhere little green shoots were visible on the trees. Frost no longer covered the hills in the distance and today I didn't blow into my hands every few minutes. The long British winter had ended. Even on this cold station not far from the city centre, I felt the change. How much nicer it must feel in the countryside. But that was the problem: I never went.

I was always struggling under the weight of work, and never

seemed to have the time. The changes in the countryside must be more pronounced. Seasons change, trees and flowers bloom, but for a city dweller these beautiful moments can be lost.

Not today; the magpie had shown on this beautiful spring morning that problems could be overcome by attempting them in small stages and with determination. I smiled at this simple truth.

High in the tree, the bird had already made half of its nest. In a few weeks it would be complete, hidden by the leaves. The bird would probably then find a mate. What did I know about magpies and nature anyway? How did magpies actually find a mate?

I had been to parks before but that was the extent of my wildlife exploration. And that was pretty dismal; I had never seen a nature reserve, gone camping in the hills, or hiked for a day or two. It all seemed like too much effort. Maybe it was time I made some effort.

This year I would try to see natural beauty and feel the peace of the hills. That's where many white folks spent their weekends, wearing boots and carrying rucksacks, looking weather-worn and fit, and heading out for long walks. I had seen them on the other side of the platform, sometimes in groups, heading in the opposite direction to the city. This get-up-and-go attitude in all kinds of weather was admirable.

Maybe that was the thing: I had to catch the train in the opposite direction. I had been going in the same direction for too long. Another resolution. Everything seems possible when the weather is warm; then work kicks in and another year passes and the resolution forgotten.

As I waited for the train, I thought there were so many

lessons one could learn from wildlife; yet most people fail to see, or to learn. Nature can pass people by their whole life; they remain stuck in the concrete jungles and stresses of the modern city. Well, I wasn't going to be one of those people any more.

Vijay Medtia, 2016

It was sad to Fanny to lose all the pleasures of spring. She had not known before what pleasures she *had* to lose in passing March and April in a town. She had not known before how much the beginnings and progress of vegetation had delighted her. What animation, both of body and mind, she had derived from watching the advance of that season which cannot, in spite of its capriciousness, be unlovely, and seeing its increasing beauties from the earliest flowers in the warmest divisions of her aunt's garden, to the opening of leaves of her uncle's plantations, and the glory of his woods. To be losing such pleasures was no trifle; to be losing them, because she was in the midst of closeness and noise, to have confinement, bad air, bad smells, substituted for liberty, freshness, fragrance, and verdure, was infinitely worse: but even these incitements to regret were feeble, compared with what arose from the conviction of being missed by her best friends, and the longing to be useful to those who were wanting her!

Jane Austen, Mansfield Park, *1814*

It's late March, and arriving at College Lake on the border of Buckinghamshire and Hertfordshire I'm immediately struck by the spectacular views. The sound of whistling ducks fills the air and children's laughter drifts up from the education centre. The sun is shining as I head down the path towards the hide closest to the visitor centre and stop at a patch of willows in flower alongside the water. Here the air is not full of the sound of birds, but an orchestra of insects.

Each spring I make a special pilgrimage to this old chalk quarry. Owned and managed by my local Wildlife Trust, it's been reclaimed by wildlife, and through careful management has become a haven especially prized for its water birds and chalk grassland plants. But today I'm not here to see either of those things. I'm here to seek out my favourite group of animals: bees!

Each bee plays its part in creating the distinctive sound which, to me, heralds spring after a long winter sadly lacking in insect life. Yet most visitors don't even notice the sound of the bees as they rush to get to the bird hides, scopes resting on their shoulders.

Most of the bees that I see on the sallow blossom are solitary. These often overlooked insects have spent the winter underground waiting to emerge on a sunny day and seek out mates and nest sites. The evidence of these nests is all around me, tiny holes visible everywhere from the side of the chalk banks to the middle of the footpaths.

There's one bee species I'm always keen to search out each

spring in the short period of time that it is active. The vivid, buff colours of *Andrena praecox* are always a joy to see. It collects pollen almost exclusively from willows and because of that emerges and nests very early in the year, dying off before many other bee species appear. This time of year is therefore very rushed for these bees, the males hyped up, zigzagging around nest sites and flowers looking for females with which to mate, and mated females hurrying about collecting pollen on the undersides of their abdomens. This pollen is moistened and, with nectar, placed in a tunnel which the female has dug herself before she carefully lays an egg, sealing it away with a saliva-like secretion before repeating the process again. Sadly, she never sees her offspring.

Queen bumblebees overwinter as adults and provide the real bass to this orchestra of bees. These enormous creatures have mated at the end of the previous summer and come out of their slumber with a great thirst for nectar. They also collect pollen with which to provision the first few workers of their colonies before becoming nest-bound and instructing their workers to collect pollen for them. There's something about the sound of a bumbling bumblebee in spring that always fills me with a warm feeling, even on the coldest of days. It gives me hope that soon the air around me will be thick with insects.

A huge queen buff-tailed bumblebee, *Bombus terrestris*, lands on the blossom in front of me. Cascades of pollen fall to the ground like snow showers coating her and everything around her. She meticulously collects the pollen on her back legs before flying off to the next flower. Closer to the ground, coltsfoot is in full bloom. This plant, which to me looks rather like a delicate version of a dandelion, flowers long before any of its leaves appear, making it quite an usual sight. However, it is beautiful in its own right, along with dandelions, and has an important role in providing nectar and pollen for a variety of more generalist bee species. One of my favourite solitary bees that often starts to appear in late March is the tawny mining bee, *Andrena fulva*. The females, as the name suggests, are black, coated with the most exquisite red/brown hairs, providing an injection of colour into the landscape.

Alongside this bee I notice *Andrena haemorrhoa*, one of my favourite springtime bees due to the vibrancy of the females' colour: they are on average a little smaller than a honey bee and are very distinctive, with a neat pile of bright red hairs on top of the thorax and a blood-red tip to the abdomen, strongly contrasting with the rest of their slate-grey bodies and yellow hind legs.

Not all solitary bees are colourful, but that doesn't make them any less important or less joyful to see. As the cloud cover starts to increase, I bend down to peer into some dandelion flowers and see the tiny heads of some all-black solitary bees peering back at me. Sheltering in the flower heads, these bees are little more than five millimetres long, yet go around carrying pollen on their hind legs between a great variety of flowers, pollinating both our wildflowers and crops.

The rain starts to fall and I head back to the car. In the few hours that I've been here I have barely made it more than a hundred metres from the visitor centre but have glimpsed into the lives of fifteen or so bee species and photographed them as they go about their busy lives, pollinating all manner of flowers, barely noticed by us. I love spring, but it will soon be over, replaced by summer and the abundance of life that it brings.

Ryan Clark, 2016

II

Loveliest of trees, the cherry now
Is hung with bloom along the bough,
And stands about the woodland ride
Wearing white for Eastertide.

Now, of my threescore years and ten,
Twenty will not come again,
And take from seventy springs a score,
It only leaves me fifty more.

And since to look at things in bloom
Fifty springs are little room,
About the woodlands I will go
To see the cherry hung with snow.

A. E. Housman, A Shropshire Lad, *1896*

What are the first signs of spring? Ask most people on the street and you'll typically get daffodils, lambs, and Easter eggs. The naturalist might go into a bit more detail, describing perhaps the first budding hazel, the first cuckoo or the reappearance of butterflies. But for me, the first real sign of spring is something most people are unaware of. For it is with the coming of spring that dragons awaken from their slumber.

Windmill Farm is a Cornwall Wildlife Trust reserve almost at the heart of the Lizard peninsula, a vast flat landscape of pasture and heathland. Its few trees and exposure to gusts racing straight from the Atlantic make it feel somehow gothic even on this fine, near-cloudless day, and the remains of the ancient windmill that gives the site its name loom over my car like a huge and ancient guardsman. A pair of ravens soar overhead, cronking and gronking as though Edgar Allan Poe might be just around the corner.

I set off down the hedgerow-hugging footpath with the standard naturalist gear of binoculars and camera, but instead of walking boots I'm wearing trainers, for if I am to find these dragons they're the perfect ally. Keeping a couple of yards to one side of the hedge, I roll each foot carefully on the soft ground. My binoculars are trained several feet away from me up the hedge, keeping a particular eye on the sunny spots close to dense clumps of vegetation.

It isn't long before this strategy is rewarded with my first dragon – although 'dragon' is a term that actually doesn't do these reptiles justice. The adder basking on the bank is exquisite, her caramel-coloured scales mixed with the classic black zigzag stripe like an organic jewel in a landscape only just beginning to turn green again. She is highly sensitive to the blundering footfalls of humans, sensing us coming through the ground like clumsy earthquakes, and the fall of my shadow over her resting spot would have sent her darting for cover at a speed remarkable for an animal with no legs. It's partly for these reasons that adders haven't been placed within the pantheon of familiar harbingers of the season, and why I've had to practice such delicate fieldcraft to see them.

But tread carefully on a warm March morning in the right sort of place and you'll hopefully be adding up lots of adders indeed – after my first sighting, I managed to see four more. Early in the day is best for seeing adders and other British reptiles, as they bask in the open, warming up for the day ahead. But as they emerge from their hibernation in spring, deep in a log pile or old rabbit warren perhaps, they're so sluggish they may as well be hungover, giving the respectful naturalist a sighting they'll remember for life.

Sleeker and slightly smaller than the females, at this time of year males can be found gliding lithely across the bracken and heather like streaks of silver cord, flicking their forked tongue in and out while on an enthusiastic trail for females ready to mate. It's with these fellas that the extremely lucky naturalist might come across the adder's dance; a misnamed activity given the two participants, twisting and coiling between each other's bodies in a mesmerising, perfectly coordinated order of rhythmic knots, are not actually a potential couple sealing their eternal bond but two blokes seeing who's more worthy of the ladies and trying to pummel each other to the ground. Less *Dirty Dancing*, more brawling drunkards outside a nightclub.

I didn't see any dancing that day at Windmill Farm, but I was made more than welcome by one of the males. Watching out for adders in a likely spot, I heard a sharp and sudden rustle from behind me. It was not the loud, well spaced-out shuffle of leaves caused by a foraging bird, nor the soft but hurried movements of a small mammal, but a long continuous drawl, like a rope being dragged through the undergrowth, of a snake on the move. I turned around to be confronted not only by a male adder slithering deftly through dead fronds of bracken, but one that had chosen to ignore all the published literature on his species' behaviour, and was rapidly slithering towards, rather than away from, me.

By the time he was about two feet directly in front of me, the continuous crackle of bracken beneath his underside hushed into silence. He sat near motionless in his perfect sun spot, the only movement being the slow, almost unperceivable flattening of his body across the ground like a deflating balloon, greedily gathering as much warmth as he could. He clearly had no idea I was there.

The thing that strikes you most when you find yourself so close to an adder is the eye. It's intense, a fiery orange with a diamond-shaped pupil of deep black. Even though he wasn't looking at me, that eye alone seemed to stare deep down into my psyche. Perhaps there was something of primal instinct in there, for it was the first time I felt slightly unnerved in the presence of the adder. It's been supposed that our widespread fear of snakes is a genetic throwback to our ancestral past in Africa, when we would have to be on the look-out for genuinely dangerous characters like the black mamba. But this feeling is brief, and easily quashed by admiration for this beautiful member of our British wildlife. I felt honoured to have been in the adder's presence as I moved back down the footpath.

We are lucky to have the adder, yet many people are either unaware or unnecessarily fearful of it. As a result, few get to marvel at what I feel is one of the greatest harbingers of spring. Just because adders aren't celebrated by nineteenth-century poets, doesn't mean they're any less wonderful than a carpet of bluebells or the song of the skylark.

For me, spring is the return of the ace of snakes.

Peter Cooper, 2016

April

Apr. 5. The frost injured the bloom of the wall-trees: covered the bloom with boughs of ivy.

Apr. 7. Tortoise keeps still in its hole.

Apr. 10. Planted two more beds of asparagus.

Apr. 15. Cucumbers swell. Tortoise sleeps on. Radishes are drawn.

Apr. 17. On this day Sir G. B. Rodney defeated the French fleet off Martinique.

Apr. 21. The tortoise heaves up the earth, & puts out its head.

Apr. 22. Tortoise comes-forth & walks around his coop: will not eat lettuce yet: goes to sleep at 4 o'clock p.m. In the hot weather last summer a flight of house-crickets were dispersed about the village: one got from the garden into my kitchen chimney, & continued there all the winter. There is now a considerable encrease & many young appear in the evening running about, & hunting for crumbs. From this circumstance it should seem that the impregnated females migrate. This is the case with ants.

Apr. 30. A sprig of *Antirrhinum cymbalaria,* the ivy-leaved Toadsflax, which was planted last year on a shady water-table [ledge or projection at top of plinth] of the wall of my house, grew at a vast rate & extended itself full nine feet: & was in perpetual bloom 'til the hard frost came. In the severity of the winter it seemed to die: but it now revives again with vigor, & shows the rudiments of flowers. When in perfection it is a lovely plant. *Lathraea sqammaria* blows in the coppice below the church-litten near the foot-bridge over the stream.

Reverend Gilbert White, The Naturalist's Journal, *1780*

The appreciation of cherry blossom or *sakura* is a national ritual in Japan. In early spring the *sakura zensen* or cherry blossom front rolls north over the Japanese islands. Celebrations are planned: the Japanese enjoy *sakuragari* (cherry blossom hunting up in the mountains); *yozakura* (looking for cherry blossom after dark); *hanamizake* (drinking sake while viewing cherry blossom); *hanami* (picknicking and singing under cherry blossoms).

While these would mostly be impractical in a British spring, our cities are indebted to the cherries that scatter pink confetti over our gridlocked cars or froth gently like bubble bath at the foot of high-rise flats. Throughout the darkest months we also enjoy the calming presence of the winter flowering cherry tree *Prunus subhirtella x autumnalis,* a slender tree with a few quickly sketched boughs and simple pale white and pink blossom. In the shelter of city gardens it flowers quietly from November onwards, reaching a muted crescendo in early spring. But it is really too polite a tree for us.

Most of our favourite Japanese cherries are *satozakura,* or temple cherries, the product of hundreds of years of cultivation. They are typically low and spreading. In the earliest flowering cherries, the blossoms often appear on naked twigs, emphasising their transient beauty. Few of the trees have fruit: most are grafted. This is a pure, sexless aesthetic.

The basic form of a Japanese flowering cherry is a large 'Y', with one of the principal limbs slightly dominant: using this shape, the monks and gardeners of Japan bred trees that evoked wind and water and moons and mountains. In Japan they may be reverentially tended, ancient trees but their life on British streets is short and testing. The low, spreading cloud shape of a Shirofugen ends up like the head of a scrubbing brush; the weeping limbs of a Shegetsu resemble a drowned bathroom spider.

Too bad about the shape. All we Brits want is blossom, lots of blossom. We always want more for our money. More chocolate, more chips, more blossom. The Japanese are careful about the use of deep pink blossom – not too much of it among the white, preferably pale and restrained – but what do they know? We love deep, deep pink cherry blossoms on streets and in gardens, front lawns, hedgerows, terraces and pots. Even the terrifying bald guy down the road with the beer gut and braces and the bull terrier loves a pink cherry.

We love the clotted-pink, supplicating boughs of a Cheal's weeping. Better yet, we love the Kanzan. In Japan the low-branching funnel shape of the Kanzan is a carefully employed flower vase, but to us it looks like a huge ice cream cone waiting to be filled with a strawberry Mr Whippy topped with jam. Its double pink flowers have as many as fifty petals: the superfluity is irresistible to our brains. The frilly flowers are like something optimistically purchased for the missus from Ann Summers. With age, the branches arch out and the Kanzan collapses into an ugly tangle but what do we care so long as it stays pink?

Kanzan is sometimes planted in roadside displays alternating with Ukon, a similar spreading ice cream cone of semi-double green-yellow flowers. The effect is a French nougat pattern of old Y-fronts and pink knickers; but perhaps the acidic harshness of the built world can only be neutralised by what is most naturally, profusely sweet and vulgar.

Cherries of all sorts have glossy grey and red bark with multiple bands round their trunks as if they had removed a score of wedding rings. Many Japanese cherries have identical boles because they are grafted onto stems of our native wild cherry or gean. In time the gean, its heart in our woodlands, becomes oppressed by its Japanese other half, who yearns for mountains and shrines. The gean grows cross and stout. The fractured Anglo-Japanese relationship shows as a swelling graft but even with this wound the marriage plods on for many years.

On its own, the gean sings the arrival of spring every bit as loud as the Japanese cherries. It is a native of our woods and it is planted commercially for timber. Not to be confused with the shrubby, sour-scented bird cherry, an old Gean can be a 90-foot, billowing spire of white blossom around Easter-time. Such a combination of size and delicacy is not plausible in the British spring. No, no: it is a mirage. The roving eye moves on, as if it had seen and dismissed the sight of an immense white elephant dancing on tiptoe among the naked branches of a distant wood. Must get the eyes tested.

In the public park the gean shows a testy wildness, suckering and setting seeds from small red fruit. It refuses to be tidy; the symmetrical cone may decide to grow additional stems or lean drunkenly towards the light. The bark-skin peels and the split trunks of old trees look like burned, exploded sausages.

On a warm, clear April day a big gean will draw the eye upwards to survey its slender blossom-tipped branches that cross-hatch the blue sky like leading in a high stained-glass window. It may also give you a sore neck.

The gean likes space and is not good for streets but the 300-year-old cultivar 'Plena' – a smaller, spreading tree with pendulous double white flowers – is commonplace. It mixes easily with the Japanese cherries which are also mostly low and wide. (The exception being Amanagawa, an unmistakable pale-pink squashed spire.) The most spectacular of the Japanese whites is the Taihaku, or great white cherry which has huge blooms like big silk flowers. It was thought to have vanished altogether in the eighteenth century, but was rediscovered in 1923, growing in a Sussex garden.

Will Cohu, Out of the Woods: The Armchair Guide to Trees, *2007*

Spring is all about change: it takes the monochrome canvas of the winter world and paints it into summer in spectacular fashion. Life flushes forth from the earth in an exhilarating show of strength, although the claws of winter can often be felt long after we thought it gone. This yearly renewal moves gradually across the country with tiny steps: the first primroses peek out from between the rocks, then the blackthorn blooms, then swallows swoop over the cliffs and the days slowly lengthen.

I once had the privilege of watching spring unfold before my eyes within the space of half a day; it was, quite simply, magical.

It was the first week of April; I had been volunteering for two weeks at the RSPB's Haweswater reserve in Cumbria and was travelling back by train to my home in Sussex. The experience had been both educational and inspiring, working with wardens who spend all year on a wet, mountainous and unforgivingly wild reserve. In Cumbria a few signs of the coming spring had already appeared and the songs of the native birds got more energetic by the day. Already several of the very first migrant birds had arrived in the area as though out of a magician's hat: pied flycatchers, swallows and wheatears made up the African lot – but they were joined by curlews that had travelled from the nearby coast to the uplands to breed. Yet despite these tentative harbingers of warmer weather, Haweswater still felt very much as though it were firmly in the clutches of Jack Frost. It rained a terrible, thick drizzle almost every day, the wind was like the breath of an ice dragon, frost encrusted the soggy ground each morning and the chill in the air seeped like a demon into my bones.

So despite having had a great experience on the reserve, I was glad to be going back to the relative warmth and dry of the south of England. The train followed a nearly exact north–south line to London from the pretty town of Penrith. When I left Cumbria the sky was its usual brooding grey self, hovering low over the mountains and stretching uninterrupted across the land until it met the north-west edge of the Yorkshire Dales. This first part of my journey showed few further signs of the arrival of spring, yet I still enjoyed the beautiful scenery of the Dales and Peak District as the train slid on its steady way past each craggy moor and smooth-sided valley.

As the train trundled slowly south into the gentle, rolling landscape of the Midlands the very air seemed to change: the sun peered through the scattering cloud and the grass quite literally looked greener; I could clearly see the hawthorns in every hedge putting forth their lime-green leaves. As we sped on through large towns and past tucked-away villages, the surrounding countryside became ever more verdant and full of life: bright flowers, mostly primroses, wild arum and dandelions, lined the verges of the roads and a few glowing marsh marigolds in the ditches were unmissable. Looking up, I spotted a couple of swallows skimming along with the urgency that all creatures have at this time of year. They were not the only birds, for when the train stopped for a few minutes at a signal post I saw herons, wrens, robins and a soaring buzzard all busily singing, feeding or displaying in one large field. I found it hard to believe that earlier that day I had been in the wet and cold and leafless Lake District – how could the spring I was now witnessing exist at the same time, in the same country, as winter?

By the time the train was just outside London some of the larger trees were in leaf too: oaks were only just bursting their buds, but elders had fully spread leaves, as did the occasional chestnut and sycamore. Over the few hundred miles I had covered on that one day the diverse signs of spring had accumulated one after the other, so that by the evening, when I reached home, spring was well and truly in charge. I had travelled through time: having started the journey in a landscape where winter was still taking its last gasps, I had ended it by fast-forwarding the year into beautiful spring. I had witnessed how the season of change sweeps northwards through our country, heralded by a few daring plants and animals in its vanguard.

Elliot Dowding, 2016

Home-Thoughts, from Abroad

I

Oh, to be in England
Now that April's there,
And who wakes in England
Sees, some morning, unaware,
That the lowest boughs and the brush-wood sheaf
Round the elm-tree bole are in tiny leaf,
While the chaffinch sings on the orchard bough
In England – now!

II

And after April, when May follows,
And the white-throat builds, and all the swallows –
Hark! where my blossomed pear-tree in the hedge
Leans to the field and scatters on the clover
Blossoms and dewdrops – at the bent spray's edge –
That 's the wise thrush: he sings each song twice over
Lest you should think he never could recapture
The first fine careless rapture!
And though the fields are rough with hoary dew,
All will be gay when noontide wakes anew
The buttercups, the little children's dower,
– Far brighter than this gaudy melon-flower!

Robert Browning, 1845

Among the meadows the buttercups in spring are as innumerable as ever and as pleasant to look upon. The petal of the buttercup has an enamel of gold; with the nail you may scrape it off, leaving still a yellow ground, but not reflecting the sunlight like the outer layer. From the centre the golden pollen covers the fingers with dust like that from the wing of a butterfly. In the branches of grass and by the gateways the germander speedwell looks like tiny specks of blue stolen, like Prometheus' fire, from the summer sky. When the mowing-grass is ripe the heads of sorrel are so thick and close that at a little distance the surface seems as if sunset were always shining red upon it. From the spotted orchis leaves in April to the honeysuckle-clover in June, and the rose and the honeysuckle itself, the meadow has changed in nothing that delights the eye. The draining, indeed, has made it more comfortable to walk about on, and some of the rougher grasses have gone from the furrows, diminishing at the same time the number of cardamine flowers; but of these there are hundreds by the side of every tiny rivulet of water, and the aquatic grasses flourish in every ditch. The meadow-farmers, dairymen, have not grubbed many hedges – only a few, to enlarge the fields, too small before, by throwing two into one. So that hawthorn and blackthorn, ash and willow, with their varied hues of green in spring, briar and bramble, with blackberries and hips later on, are still there as in the old, old time. Bluebells, violets, cowslips – the same old favourite flowers – may be found on the mounds or sheltered nearby. The meadow-farmers have dealt mercifully with the hedges, because they know that for shade in heat and shelter in storm the cattle resort to them. The hedges – yes, the hedges, the very synonym of Merry England – are yet there, and long may they remain. Without hedges England would not be England. Hedges, thick and high, and full of flowers, birds, and living creatures, of shade and flecks of sunshine dancing up and down the bark of the trees – I love their very thorns. You do not know how much there is in hedges.

We have still the woods, with here and there a forest, the beauty of the hills, and the charm of the winding brooks. I never see roads, or horses, men, or anything when I get beside a brook. There is the grass, and the wheat, the clouds, the delicious sky, and the wind, and the sunlight which falls on the heart like a song. It is the same, the very same, only I think it is brighter and more lovely now than it was twenty years ago.

Along the footpath we travel slowly; you cannot walk fast very long in a footpath; no matter how rapidly at first, you soon lessen your page, and country people always walk slowly. The stiles – how stupidly they are put together. For years and years every one who has passed them, as long as man can remember, has grumbled at them; yet there they are still, with the elms reaching high above, and cows gazing over – cows that look so powerful, but so peacefully yield the way. They are a better shape than the cattle of the ancient time, less lanky, and with fewer corners; the lines, to talk in yachtsman's language, are finer. Roan is a colour that contrasts well with meadows and hedges. The horses are finer, both cart-horse and nag. Approaching the farmsteads, there are hay-ricks, but there are fewer corn-ricks. Instead of the rows on rows, like the conical huts of a savage town, there are but a few, sometimes none. So many are built in the fields and threshed there 'to rights', as the bailiff would say. It is not needful to have them near home or keep them, now the threshing-machine has stayed the flail and emptied the barns. Perhaps these are the only two losses to those who look at things and mete them with the eye – the corn-ricks and the barns. The corn-ricks were very characteristic, but even now you may see plenty if you look directly after the harvest. The barns are going by degrees, passing out of the life of farming; let us hope that some of them will be converted into silos, and so saved.

At the farmsteads themselves there are considerations for and against. On the one hand, the house and the garden is much tidier, less uncouth; there are flowers, such as geraniums, standard roses, those that are favourites in towns; and the unsightly and unhealthy middens and pools of muddy water have disappeared from beside the gates. But the old flowers and herbs are gone, or linger neglected in corners, and somehow the gentle touch of time has been effaced. The house has got a good deal away from farming. It is on the farm but disconnected. It is a residence, not a farmhouse. Then you must consider that it is more healthy, sweeter, and better for those who live in it. From a little distance the old effect is obtainable. One thing only I must protest against, and that is the replacing of tiles with slates. The old red tiles of the farmhouses are as natural as leaves; they harmonise with the trees and the hedges, the grass, the wheat, and the ricks. But slates are wrong. In new houses, even farmhouses, it does not matter so much; the owners cannot be found fault with for using the advantages of modern times. On old houses where tiles were once, to put slates is an offence, nothing less. Every one who passes exclaims against it. Tiles tone down and become at home; they nestle together, and look as if you could be happily drowsy and slumber under them. They are to a house what leaves are to a tree, and leaves turn reddish or brown in the autumn. Upon the whole, with the exception of the slates – the hateful slates – the farmsteads are improved, for they have lost a great deal that was uncouth and even repulsive, which was slurred over in old pictures or omitted, but which was there.

The new cottages are ugly with all their ornamentation; their false gables, impossible porches, absurd windows, are distinctly repellent. They are an improvement in a sanitary sense, and we are all glad of that, but we cannot like the buildings. They are of no style or time; only one thing is certain about them – they are *not* English. Fortunately there are plenty of old cottages, hundreds of them (they show little or no sign of disappearing), and these can be chosen instead. The villages are to outward appearance very much as they used to be, but the people are very different. In manners, conversation, and general tone there is a great change. It is, indeed, the people who have altered more than the surface of the country. Hard as the farmer may work, and plough and sow with engine and drill, the surface of the land does not much vary; but the farmer himself and the farmer's man are quite another race to what they were. Perhaps it was from this fact that the impression grew up that modern agriculture has polished away all the distinctive characteristics of the country. But it has not done so any more than it has removed the hills. The truth is, as I have endeavoured to explain, innovations so soon become old in the fields. The ancient earth covers them with her own hoar antiquity, and their newness disappears. They have already become so much a part of the life of the country that it seems as if they had always been there, so easily do they fit in, so easily does the eye accept them.

Intrinsically there is nothing used in modern agriculture less symmetrical than what was previously employed. The flails were the simplest of instruments, and were always seen with the same accompaniment – the interior of a barn. The threshing-machine is certainly not less interesting; it works in the open air, often with fine scenic surroundings, and the number of people with it impart vivacity. In reaping with the reaping-hook there were more men in the wheat, but the reaping-machine is not without colour. Scythes are not at all pleasant things; the mowing-machine is at least no worse. As for the steam-plough, it is very interesting to watch. All these fit in with trees and hedges, fields and woods, as well, and in some cases in a more striking manner than the old instruments. The surface of the ground presents more varied colours even than before, and the sunlight produces rich effect. Nor have all the ancient aspects disappeared as supposed – quite the reverse. In the next field to the steam-plough the old ploughs drawn by horses may be seen at work, and barns still stand, and the old houses. In hill districts oxen are yet yoked to the plough, the scythe and reaping-hook are often seen at work, and, in short, the old and the new so shade and blend together that you can hardly say where one begins and the other ends. That there are many, very many things concerning agriculture and country life whose disappearance is to be regretted I have often pointed out, and having done so, I feel that I can with the more strength affirm that in its natural beauty the country is as lovely now as ever.

It is, I venture to think, a mistake on the part of some who depict country scenes on canvas that they omit these modern aspects, doubtless under the impression that to admit them would impair the pastoral scene intended to be conveyed. So many pictures and so many illustrations seem to proceed upon the assumption that steam-plough and reaping-machine do not exist, that the landscape contains nothing but what it did a hundred years ago. These sketches are often beautiful, but they lack the force of truth and reality. Every one who has been fifty miles into the country, if only by rail, knows while looking at them that they are not real. You feel that there is something wanting, you do not know what. That something is the hard, perhaps angular fact which at once makes the sky above it appear likewise a fact. Why omit fifty years from the picture? That is what it usually means – fifty years left out; and somehow we feel as we gaze that these fields and these skies are not of our day. The actual fields, the actual machines, the actual men and women (how differently dressed to the conventional pictorial costumes!) would prepare the mind to see and appreciate the colouring, the design, the beauty – what, for lack of a better expression, may be called the soul of the picture – far more than forgotten, and nowadays even impossible accessories. For our sympathy is not with them, but with the things of our own time.

Richard Jefferies, The Life of the Fields, *1884*

The sound infiltrated my consciousness slowly at first. It took me a second or two to tune in to the insistent buzzing, more mechanical than natural; and another few seconds to realise what I was listening to: one of the rarest birds I have ever come across in Britain.

I've always been captivated by warblers. Yet as a young birder, growing up on the outskirts of London, I hardly ever came across them. This was not, as I then thought, because they are particularly rare – they are not. It was simply because in those days I didn't listen to, learn, or appreciate the importance of birdsong. I didn't *see* warblers because you usually don't – they are much easier to identify by their distinctive songs.

Nowadays, on a typical walk around my local patch on the edge of the Somerset Levels on a fine spring morning, I might hear around fifty different warblers of at least half a dozen species. But I usually see just three or four – and even then, I only get a brief glimpse before they melt back into the reeds or disappear into the dense woodland canopy.

Fortunately their songs are (mostly) pretty distinctive. The easiest by far are the chiffchaff, usually the earliest to arrive, which conveniently sings its own name, and the resident Cetti's warbler. This elusive bird is as loud as it is skulking, and shouts its explosive song from deep inside the dense thickets in every month of the year.

Early April brings the first blackcap, with a melodious, fluty song like a speeded-up blackbird; and then the willow warbler, whose plaintive descant of silvery notes runs down the scale like a mountain stream. Hearing my first willow warbler of the spring is always a special moment for me. Unlike the chiffchaffs and blackcaps, which overwinter in southern Europe, Spain or even here in southern England, these tiny birds have flown all the way from sub-Saharan Africa – a journey of five thousand miles or more.

The willow warbler is swiftly followed by four more long-distance migrants. Two of these chunter from the reedbeds, the more plodding, repetitive reed warbler outshone by its more extrovert, excitable cousin, the sedge warbler. A lone whitethroat nests in the brambles along the path, occasionally launching himself into the air on long, slender wings, to reinforce his claim to his thorny territory. And one or two garden warblers – whose song sounds like an even faster, more rambling version of the blackcap's – occasionally sing from the wooded drove.

And that, usually, is that: eight species of warbler should be enough for anyone, surely. But this year was a very special one, with two new warblers appearing on my patch for the very first time.

One day in the middle of April, I was walking along when I heard a strange sound, rather like a fishing reel being unwound at speed, or perhaps a very loud insect. This comparison is apt, as it was a grasshopper warbler; the only British bird whose common and scientific names derive from an invertebrate: it belongs to the genus *Locustella*.

Grasshopper warblers are skulking little birds, like a streaky version of the reed warbler, and rarely show themselves – though I did manage to get a reasonable view one day, as the bird perched momentarily in a low bush above the reeds.

A couple of weeks later the bird had stopped singing, and I assumed it had gone; when a friend informed me that he thought he had heard it again. But as I stood and listened to the monotonous buzz, something was bothering me. The tone was somehow different – less metallic and more 'wooden' – and the pitch seemed lower.

Then it dawned on me: I was listening to the grasshopper warbler's much rarer cousin, Savi's warbler. Named after Paolo Savi, the nineteenth-century Italian scientist who discovered the species, Savi's warblers are incredibly rare in Britain, with only a handful arriving to sing in our southern reedbeds each spring. Yet here was one on my local patch.

Over the next couple of weeks I visited at dawn and dusk, when Savi's do most of their singing. I only glimpsed it once: a brief view of a plain brown bird, remarkably like a reed warbler. No wonder it took ornithologists so long to realise this was a new and separate species.

Then it simply stopped singing. Either it had flown away, or had found a female and settled down to breed – I couldn't tell. But I am hoping that Savi's warbler will now, after several failed attempts, colonise Britain permanently as a breeding bird. Maybe, in a decade's time, that strange, buzzing song will be as part of the Somerset landscape as the booming of another recent arrival, the bittern.

But whatever should happen I'll never forget the joy of hearing no fewer than ten different kinds of warbler singing on my local patch, during that unforgettable 'warbler spring'.

Stephen Moss, 2016

Vernal Birds of Passage. The earlier or later appearance of our Spring Birds may be found to arise from accidental vicissitudes of the season in those countries from whence they come, and viewed in this light, the time of their arrival becomes an interesting phenomena to note down. Generally speaking, they arrive at the following times, on an average of many years:

Wryneck	Middle of March.
Smallest Willow Wren	March 25.
House Swallow	April 15.
Martin	April 20.
Sand Martin	April 20.
Blackcap	April 17.
Nightingale	April 10.
Cuckoo	April 21.
Yellow Willow Wren	April 20.
Whitethroat	April 16.
Redstart	April 16.
Night Plover or Stone Curlew	March 27.
Grasshopper Lark	April 15.
Swift	May 9.
Lesser Red Sparrow	April 30.
Corn Crake or Land Rail	April 25.
Largest Willow Wren	End of April.
Fern Owl	May 20.
Flycatcher	May 3.

Other birds, Water Wagtails for instance, who only make partial migrations, are more uncertain in their times of appearance.

Thomas Furly Forster, The Pocket Encyclopaedia of Natural Phenomena, *published 1827*

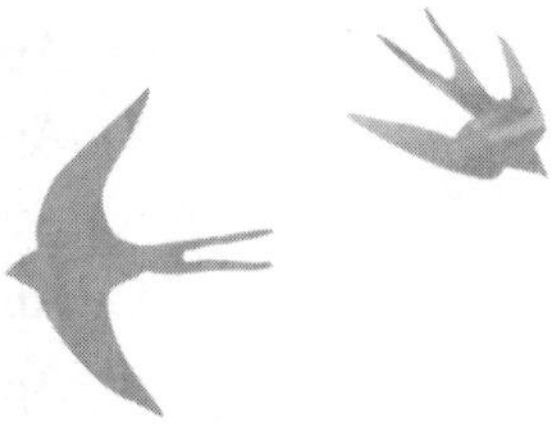

Beyond a quiet road bridge near Builth, Powys, a steep, shallow stream joins the Wye. If you peer down you'll notice the clarity of the water, the rocks and wood on the riverbed, and living roots reaching into the flow for sustenance. The waters are full of calcium and magnesium ions, while dead leaves, washed from upstream, lie heavy on the bedrock; allochthonous material, key to nutrient cycling and food web dynamics. Rich stuff.

This place, this rivers-meet, is perfect for white-clawed crayfish, the UK's largest native freshwater invertebrate. The main channel runs north to south, and crays seek shelter here from strong sun, east to west. Sensitive to temperature, they also love oxygen. They'll survive both running and still water, canals and quarry lakes, but like living litmus tests of alkaline waters they flourish in places like this, on calcareous and weathered rock. Here, they graze on aquatic green algae, charophytes to boost their calcium levels at moulting time. Here, when winter snow melts and April showers fall, the shallow meets the deep with such force one can hear it long before it is seen. They thrive on the oxygen-rich froth of hydrological turbulence. So do we.

Rivers are maps for all living things, natural diviners of place. Freshwater travels from higher to lower ground, to estuaries and beyond, and the rivers' strong presence in landscape changes only slowly over time. They guide us through life, with not a roadmap in sight, their angiological patterns etched deep within our minds.

The female crayfish here will have mated with larger-clawed males in autumn, and have protected those fertilised eggs through winter spates in submerged, muddy burrows under thicker riparian vegetation. After the eggs hatch, the young have remained bonded with their mother, attached to her broader abdomen, through all the perils of spring floods, until eventually they separate and live an independent life in early summer. They become active at night to hunt, and, as well as algae, they'll eat carrion, macro-invertebrates, worms and snails, small fish and larger aquatic plants. To a white-clawed cray, turbidity is like smog. Nothing much likes smog. Crayfish love clarity. So do we.

The river-story continues. Freshly hewn stones and grit, gifted from the hills, sink into the depths. Twenty widths or so downstream, the waters are fully mixed. Any silt – though not much, one hopes, at this point in a river's journey – is carried down to fertile plains. Meanwhile, up-flow, hidden signs exist at rivers-meets legible only to fish like Atlantic salmon, as they return to higher spawning grounds. Confluences are their signs, their directional arrows. *Here, where the crayfish hunt, swim left. Now, swim right. Right again. Now lay eggs to hatch and eventually tumble back to the ocean.*

These rivers-meets, so often ignored, could instead be our meeting places, to bring our young in celebration or mourning of all that life involves. Light, dark, where geologies blend and fresh air is released in tiny bubbles for us to draw in deep. Let's paint beautiful signs in celebration of the life that highlands bring to lowlands, symbols of respect and union. Let's paint the rivers' names, pay tribute to the headwaters and oceans they join together in ribbons. Use nearby boulders or windfall oak, gable ends, whatever suits. In spring, when the sun begins to burn off the cloud and creatures emerge from their winter quiet, let's draw all manner of beautiful beings that live in and around the river: a blaze of shape, form and colour.

The confluence on the Wye is a good place to make a sign. It's a great spot for a picnic, too – pink lemonade moments under a canopy of beech and alder, newly unfurling leaves in spring – a time which grants that particular lightness of being from breathing in soft air. I'd choose a mother cray to represent this rivers-meet, with brood bonded to her abdomen. This would be our mutual place: shared, loved, with potential to begin a beautiful evolution of rivers-meet signs. This is where I bring my daughter.

From the rivers-meets, on riparian paths, reconnected to nature, we could navigate upstream . . . downstream . . . to the bigger swell or finer flow. Our compass becomes a story. We remember stories and we follow signs, just as the salmon do. We know the sanctity of home, of clarity and sustenance, like the crayfish.

North of alder grove, south of small-leaved lime, east of broken willow, west of river cliffs. Here at the confluence, where the dead oak tumbles to nurse young life, when spring merges to summer, releasing them into adulthood. This is where the crayfish live. Home.

Ginny Battson, 2016

Here bygynneth the Book of the Tales of Caunterbury

Whan that Aprill, with his shoures soote
The droghte of March hath perced to the roote
And bathed every veyne in swich licour,
Of which vertu engendred is the flour;
Whan Zephirus eek with his sweete breeth
Inspired hath in every holt and heeth
The tendre croppes, and the yonge sonne
Hath in the Ram his halfe cours yronne,
And smale foweles maken melodye,
That slepen al the nyght with open eye-
(So priketh hem Nature in hir corages);
Thanne longen folk to goon on pilgrimages
And palmeres for to seken straunge strondes
To ferne halwes, kowthe in sondry londes;
And specially from every shires ende
Of Engelond, to Caunterbury they wende,
The hooly blisful martir for to seke
That hem hath holpen, whan that they were seeke.

Geoffrey Chaucer, The Canterbury Tales, *1386–89*

Sitting by the coastal path on the top of Portland, I can trace Chesil Beach along the Dorset coast until it disappears into Devon. The harsh winter landscape has melted away, its grey-churned sea and stormy skies now sparkling with warmth as the sun highlights the turquoise in the tips of the waves.

Today the bluster is fresh but tinged with something else: excitement. New arrivals are here, promising a great season to come.

Little terns arrive as early as April and make the great beach their home for the next few months. Their soft white form contrasts with their night-sky mask and pointed wings, making it a handsome bird. This rare breeding migrant has a special place in the heart of Chesil, where it doesn't need to compete with tourists for its designated patch on the pebbles.

When they arrive, many simply wait and watch the soap opera play out. It starts predictably: in they come, and there is courting to be done. There's nothing like a fish supper to impress a female little tern. Chattering for attention and comically sidling up to the female, the male presents his silvery sand-eel gift. There is ceremonial behaviour to be observed; it is an incredibly formal affair. Sometimes the clever females seem to let the males think they are ready to mate, then whip the fish away and head off with a free lunch.

Eventually, after all the bowing and dancing, they settle down to lay precious eggs on the not-so-cosy Chesil pebbles. Their camouflage is so superb that people have been known to walk right by their nests and not see them. Predators manage to locate them, though: hedgehogs sometimes amble along the beach to enjoy a snack, while a cunning fox may use the cover of darkness to test the electric fence that guards them. Before spring is over, tiny speckled chicks will be tumbling unsteadily around the pebbles, visible only to the keenest eyes. When you see their vulnerability, you hope with all your heart these little creatures will survive the summer.

But there are even more surprising beach dwellers. On the bright early mornings in spring I spot them – or rather, ever alert, they spot me – and I catch a glimpse of a long-limbed hare as it bounds away down the beach. In the less frequented areas of Chesil they breed and have their young, but they remain a mystery and a glimpse is all you get. It's reassuring to know that this elusive countryside creature can find a haven here on the coast, away from dangerous farm machinery. There will always be a bit of mystery and oddity to this unique place.

Melissa Spiers, 2016

It was a threatening, misty morning, but mild. We set off after dinner from Eusemere. Mrs Clarkson went a short way with us, but turned back. The wind was furious, and we thought we must have returned. We first rested in the large boat-house, then under a furze bush opposite Mr Clarkson's. Saw the plough going in the field. The wind seized our breath. The Lake was rough. There was a boat by itself floating in the middle of the bay below Water Millock. We rested again in the Water Millock Lane. The hawthorns are black and green, the birches here and there greenish, but there is yet more of purple to be seen on the twigs. We got over into a field to avoid some cows – people working. A few primroses by the roadside – woodsorrel flowers, the anemone, scentless violets, strawberries, and that starry, yellow flower which Mrs C. calls pile wort. When we were in the woods beyond Gowbarrow Park we saw a few daffodils close to the water-side. We fancied that the lake had floated the seeds ashore, and that the little colony had so sprung up. But as we went along there were more and yet more; and at last, under the boughs of the trees, we saw that there was a long belt of them along the shore, about the breadth of a country turnpike road. I never saw daffodils so beautiful.

They grew among the mossy stones about and about them; some rested their heads upon these stones as on a pillow for weariness; and the rest tossed and reeled and danced, and seemed as if they verily laughed with the wind, that blew upon them over the lake; they looked so gay, ever glancing, ever changing. This wind blew directly over the lake to them. There was here and there a little knot, and a few stragglers a few yards higher up; but they were so few as not to disturb the simplicity, unity, and life of that one busy highway.

We rested again and again. The bays were stormy, and we heard the waves at different distances, and in the middle of the water, like the sea. Rain came on – we were wet when we reached Luff's, but we called in. Luckily all was cheerless and gloomy, so we faced the storm – we *must* have been wet if we had waited – put on dry clothes at Dobson's. I was very kindly treated by a young woman, the landlady looked sour, but it is her way. She gave us a goodish supper, excellent ham and potatoes. We paid 7/- when we came away. William was sitting by a bright fire when I came downstairs. He soon made his way to the library, piled up in a corner of the window. He brought out a volume of Enfield's *Speaker,* another miscellany, and an odd volume of Congreve's plays. We had a glass of warm rum and water. We enjoyed ourselves and wished for Mary. It rained and blew, when we went to bed. N.B. Deer in Gowbarrow Park like skeletons.

Thursday, 15 April 1802

Dorothy Wordsworth, The Grasmere Journals, *published 1897*

The beauty of the view, the first view of the village, coming down by the Brooms this evening was indescribable. The brilliant golden poplar spires shone in the evening light like flames against the dark hill side of the Old Forest and the blossoming fruit trees, the torch trees of Paradise blazed with a transparent green and white lustre up the dingle in the setting sunlight. The village is in a blaze of fruit blossom. Clyro is at its loveliest. What more can be said?

Sunday, 14 April 1871

Reverend Francis Kilvert, Kilvert's Diary 1870–79

In the city the day was warming up. In the past week spring had fallen like a benediction, the sun warming the grimy pavements, charming weed shoots through the cracks and drawing blind thistles up under the tarmac in unlikely bulges. The grass had begun to grow, re-greening the gardens, the parks and the verges with their cargos of litter and cuckoo spit and grime. Even the waste ground between the old bingo hall and the railway line, strewn with faded estate agents' boards, rotting sleepers and huge wooden drums once wound with cable, even these abandoned corners were warmed by the spring sunshine and had become rank and dizzy with life.

On Leasow Road the cherries blushed cornelian or dappled the pavement below with palest pink. Outside some lucky houses magnolias were opening their miraculous, waxy blooms, their fallen petals like slivers of soap on the pavements beneath, bruising to brown with time, and feet. On earthy islets in crazy-paved front gardens specimen roses unfurled new, red leaves, while from verge, bed and central reservation nodded the municipal daffs.

Now the Somali postman found himself shadowed on his rounds by wood pigeons' dozy coos, while on sunny afternoons starlings clicked and chattered from the aerials like avian telegraph operators sending news about each street's coming and goings on the wires. And along the long, unlovely high road the estates were once again jubilant with birds. Robins sang riotously from street lamp, sill and gutter; blackbirds spilled their song down into the tangled yards behind the high-rise blocks. Pigeons jostled the windowsills above grimy shopfronts, and at sunset their assemblies were hosted by the sun-warmed roofs.

The spring sunshine brought a new mood of optimism everywhere it fell. Workmen left doors and windows open, causing all but the most stubbornly unmusical to fall into step with their radios as they passed. Women, bound by the same circadian rhythm, swapped gloves for sunglasses in their everyday handbags. And at the end of each school day the kids streamed screaming out of the gates, eager not for home and TV, but just to be out, free, in the burgeoning world.

Melissa Harrison, Clay, *2013*

For countless generations, the cuckoo has been the best-known and most eagerly awaited harbinger of spring. Many of the legends concerning the time of its arrival were connected with foretelling the kind of weather to be expected during the coming summer, information of great importance for estimating the timing and magnitude of the harvest. Before people had calendars, the arrival of the cuckoo was also an invaluable point around which to set the farming programme, as its first appearance varies by little more than a week or so from year to year.

It was widely held that the cuckoo actually brought the spring weather with it, so if it came with a fine warm spell, that sort of weather would continue. The weather was of vital importance to our ancestors, and many believed that it was decreed and sent by a deity. This deity manifested itself in many different ways all over the world, but in almost every case it needed to be appeased by offerings or sacrifices. Over the years, the regular observance of these rituals grew into the tradition of spring festivals. These would celebrate the renewal of vegetation and the return of the sun, the triumph of life over death and the hopes of a plentiful harvest to come. And the form they often took was cuckoo festivals.

There were many such festivals in Britain, and one of the last to survive was the Towednack cuckoo festival in Cornwall. This was always held on the Sunday nearest to 28 April, which itself was close to the usual date of the cuckoo's arrival. The festival was held to commemorate a legend about an old man who grew tired of waiting for winter to end. Impatient as he was, he decided to invite friends to celebrate spring, even though it hadn't arrived yet. As he lit a large log fire for them, a cuckoo flew out of a hollow log, and was immediately followed by warm summery weather.

Perhaps because the cuckoo arrives at a time of year when many different sorts of spring festivals take place, there are quite a few amusing stories about the bird's involvement in the festivities. In Herefordshire, it was said to make a beeline for Orleton Fair on 23 April, where it would buy a horse to sell at Brompton Bruan Fair. In Worcestershire, they claimed that the bird never missed Tenbury Fair on 20 April, and was never heard after Pershore Fair on 26 June. The reason given was that the bird would buy a horse at Pershore then ride away for another year.

Traditional annual dates for the arrival of the cuckoo are different all over Europe. In the South of France, it was said that the cuckoo's song would be heard during the festival of the Feast of St Benedict (21 March). If it had not begun to sing by 25 March (Annunciation Day), then it was assumed the bird must either have been killed or have frozen to death. In Normandy it was expected to arrive on 1 April, while in parts of Germany the peasants looked for its arrival on the feast of St Valerian and St Tiburtius (14 April), the same day as the nightingale was expected. In the north of Norway its arrival was fixed for 1 May, the feast of St Philip and St James.

By far the most elaborate of the folk ceremonies constructed around the arrival of the cuckoo took place in Pragança in Portugal. Here, a cuckoo was captured and set on a cart with two old ladies, one of whom was spinning and the other weaving. The cart would then be paraded through the streets with an escort of three hundred horsemen.

Another well-known aspect of cuckoo lore was the belief that the bird was able to foretell the future. In Yorkshire, children used to play a game in which they danced round a cherry tree singing:

Cuckoo, cuckoo, cherry-tree,
Good bird, prithee, tell to me
How many years I am to see.

Each child would then take it in turns to shake the tree, and the number of cherries which fell was said to correspond to the number of years they would live. A similar tradition existed in the west of Scotland, where it was thought that the number of calls a cuckoo made the first time it was heard predicted how many years the hearer had to live.

Peter Tate, Flights of Fancy: Birds in Myth, Legend and Superstition, *2007*

In one little corner of Berkshire's Moor Copse the ground flora is putting on as varied a display as one might see in a shop window, as if preparing for a one-stop field guide photography session. The show begins just a few paces in from the wood's edge, where I lose myself in a reverie of petals and sunlight.

This is the sort of British wildwood I love. The endless, primordial wildwood of myth and legend is, of course, long gone (if it was ever here at all) but there are pockets of forest here and there that retain a sense of timelessness. To delve into these woods is to enter another realm where sound and weather and seasons differ from the world outside. The pace of superficial change in a single wood during springtime can be startling; but take the long view and walking in the woods can be like tapping into deep time: a faraway place unchanged from spring to spring and from age to age.

This is the disorientating magic of the woods, for in reality woodland need only have been around for 400 years to be classified as 'ancient', and only fourteen patches or so in the entire country are larger than a square mile. The here and now of woodland Britain is certainly not what it was – even as the cycling of the seasons feels misleadingly eternal.

Still, almost nothing marks out those seasons like plants. As the year turns, their full glories exist mostly *in potentia*: a bud, a stem, a seed, a dry frame of twigs, all waiting for the tilt of the earth's axis to point them once more towards the sun. With each nightfall and sunrise we lean a little closer. The appearance of small, delicate flowers is one of the first signs that the year is truly waxing, that light and colour are returning to overwrite the comparatively subtle, monochrome hues of winter.

This time two years ago the light and colour of the plants at Moor Copse was still, to me, an abstract haze. I barely knew the name of a single wildflower. The list of plants of which I know very little is still lengthy, to say the least, but after a few years of slowly accumulating knowledge I'm at least able to greet the more common woodland flowers, like a gathering of old friends. For who could remain a stranger when faced with such full-colour glories? The yellows of celandine, primroses and archangel; blues and purples from the orchids, violets and bluebells; the bright pink of 'red' campion; whites of anemones, stitchwort, sorrel and ramsons; and the fresh, cool green of wood spurge.

Early purple orchids, indeed any orchids, are a particular revelation to the novice student of sylvan botany. Something so architecturally remarkable, picked out in deep pink and purple, is not supposed to unfold from the dank cool of the leaf litter. Surely nothing this exotic could persist in the British countryside. Or consider the wood anemone, bright morning star of the forest floor. There's almost nothing else in nature so crisp linen-fresh, so purely white. Other whites are path lights guiding the way to a feast for all the senses, whether the deeply pungent garlic scent from a drift of ramsons or the apple-skin-and-rhubarb sourness of a wood sorrel leaf I nibble on as I walk.

Many of these are as easily seen in banks of undisturbed, mature hedgerows, in the dappled light of oaks and ash and a diverse understory. This is telling. Today's woodland is a risky place for a wildflower: over-shaded or over-browsed, it is a place either over-managed for plantation or under-managed to the point of neglect. Are wooded road verges and old hedges going the same way, lost to convenience, tidiness or cost-cutting? It took a walk through a carefully tended Wildlife Trust reserve to see such a fantastic display of spring flowers, but surely we should see dazzling riots of colour wherever we look at the height of spring?

Flowering plants are species as wild as any bird or butterfly, and it isn't possible to conceive of spring without them. Perhaps the rewilding of each of us, each wood, and even spring itself, should begin with wildflowers, freeing the new-old spirit of the season that persists in fragments to burst out into every corner of the countryside.

Chris Foster, 2016

Meanwhile the work of the farm was toward, and every day gave us more ado to dispose of what itself was doing. For after the long dry skeltering wind of March and part of April, there had been a fortnight of soft wet; and when the sun came forth again, hill and valley, wood and meadow, could not make enough of him. Many a spring have I seen since then, but never yet two springs alike, and never one so beautiful. Or was it that my love came forth and touched the world with beauty?

The spring was in our valley now; creeping first for shelter shyly in the pause of the blustering wind. There the lambs came bleating to her, and the orchis lifted up, and the thin dead leaves of clover lay for the new ones to spring through. There the stiffest things that sleep, the stubby oak, and the saplin'd beech, dropped their brown defiance to her, and prepared for a soft reply.

While her over-eager children (who had started forth to meet her, through the frost and shower of sleet), catkin'd hazel, gold-gloved withy, youthful elder, and old woodbine, with all the tribe of good hedge-climbers (who must hasten while haste they may) – was there one of them that did not claim the merit of coming first?

There she stayed and held her revel, as soon as the fear of frost was gone; all the air was a fount of freshness, and the earth of gladness, and the laughing waters prattled of the kindness of the sun.

But all this made it much harder for us, plying the hoe and rake, to keep the fields with room upon them for the corn to tiller. The winter wheat was well enough, being sturdy and strong-sided; but the spring wheat and the barley and the oats were overrun by ill weeds growing faster. Therefore, as the old saying is, –

'Farmer, that thy wife may thrive,
Let not burr and burdock wive;
And if thou wouldst keep thy son,
See that bine and gith have none.'

So we were compelled to go down the field and up it, striking in and out with care where the green blades hung together, so that each had space to move in and to spread its roots abroad. And I do assure you now, though you may not believe me, it was harder work to keep John Fry, Bill Dadds, and Jem Slocomb all in a line and all moving nimbly to the tune of my own tool, than it was to set out in the morning alone, and hoe half an acre by dinner-time. For, instead of keeping the good ash moving, they would for ever be finding something to look at or to speak of, or at any rate, to stop with; blaming the shape of their tools perhaps, or talking about other people's affairs; or, what was most irksome of all to me, taking advantage as married men, and whispering jokes of no excellence about my having, or having not, or being ashamed of a sweetheart. And this went so far at last that I was forced to take two of them and knock their heads together; after which they worked with a better will.

When we met together in the evening round the kitchen chimney-place, after the men had had their supper and their heavy boots were gone, my mother and Eliza would do their very utmost to learn what I was thinking of. Not that we kept any fire now, after the crock was emptied; but that we loved to see the ashes cooling, and to be together. At these times Annie would never ask me any crafty questions (as Eliza did), but would sit with her hair untwined, and one hand underneath her chin, sometimes looking softly at me, as much as to say that she knew it all and I was no worse off than she. But strange to say my mother dreamed not, even for an instant, that it was possible for Annie to be thinking of such a thing. She was so very good and quiet, and careful of the linen, and clever about the cookery and fowls and bacon-curing, that people used to laugh, and say she would never look at a bachelor until her mother ordered her. But I (perhaps from my own condition and the sense of what it was) felt no certainty about this, and even had another opinion, as was said before.

Often I was much inclined to speak to her about it, and put her on her guard against the approaches of Tom Faggus; but I could not find how to begin, and feared to make a breach between us; knowing that if her mind was set, no words of mine would alter it; although they needs must grieve her deeply. Moreover, I felt that, in this case, a certain homely Devonshire proverb would come home to me; that one, I mean, which records that the crock was calling the kettle smutty. Not, of course, that I compared my innocent maid to a highwayman; but that Annie might think her worse, and would be too apt to do so, if indeed she loved Tom Faggus. And our Cousin Tom, by this time, was living a quiet and godly life; having retired almost from the trade (except when he needed excitement, or came across public officers), and having won the esteem of all whose purses were in his power.

Perhaps it is needless for me to say that all this time while my month was running – or rather crawling, for never month went so slow as that with me – neither weed, nor seed, nor cattle, nor my own mother's anxiety, nor any care for my sister, kept me from looking once every day, and even twice on a Sunday, for any sign of Lorna. For my heart was ever weary; in the budding valleys, and by the crystal waters, looking at the lambs in fold, or the heifers on the mill, labouring in trickled furrows, or among the beaded blades; halting fresh to see the sun lift over the golden-vapoured ridge; or doffing hat, from sweat of brow, to watch him sink in the low gray sea; be it as it would of day, of work, or night, or slumber, it was a weary heart I bore, and fear was on the brink of it.

All the beauty of the spring went for happy men to think of; all the increase of the year was for other eyes to mark. Not a sign of any sunrise for me from my fount of life, not a breath to stir the dead leaves fallen on my heart's Spring.

R. D. Blackmore, Lorna Doone: A Romance of Exmoor, *1869*

Purple-chequered snake's head fritillaries on their delicate, curved stems are a sight to behold. Heralding the arrival of spring, a traditionally managed water meadow full of these lovely flowers brings joy to the heart, tinged with sadness at how much of our classic country landscape has been lost. Once commonplace, the snake's head fritillary is now one of the rarest plants in the country. Although they thrive in places like Iffley Meadows in the centre of Oxford, they are barely clinging on elsewhere in the face of modern farming techniques.

Iffley Meadows is managed by the Berkshire, Buckinghamshire and Oxfordshire Wildlife Trust and is one of the best places in the country to see snake's head fritillaries. A visit in April, either as part of a guided tour or by just wandering down the riverbank until you stumble across the reserve entrance, is a breathtaking experience. Purple-, pink- and even white-chequered flowers, heads down and necks arched, gently nod above their lush green surroundings. The spring sunshine glints on their silvery scales, making the blooms glow and sparkle. Birds busy themselves in the surrounding reeds, butterflies flit from flower to flower, drooping willow trees rustle in the gentle breeze and swans glide up and down the sparkling river. It is a small piece of heaven.

A mere 500 flowers were recorded in the meadows before BBOWT took over the site in 1983, but careful management has seen this number steadily increase in recent years so that in the spring of 2015 just under 90,000 flowers were recorded in the annual count. The plants thrive because the site is maintained as a traditional water meadow, cutting for hay in July so the nutrient levels stay low, grazing cattle through the autumn and early winter to keep sedges and rushes at bay and allowing the fields to flood to retain the soil's dampness.

Fritillaria meleagris is the county flower of Oxfordshire, a member of the lily family and the UK's only native fritillary species. It stands 15 to 40 centimetres tall and is one of the earliest floral spectacles each year, in bloom between April and May. The words 'fritillary' and 'fritillaria' come from the Latin *fritillus*, 'dice box', referring to its chequerboard pattern, and *meleagris* means speckled and likens it to a spotted guinea fowl. Other names for the plant include chequered lily, dead man's bell, frog cup, fraucup and leper's bell, as their bell-shaped flowers resemble the bells worn by lepers in the Middle Ages.

Snake's head fritillaries used to be found in water meadows right across southern and central England. Ford, a village in Buckinghamshire, was famous for its meadows full of fraucups, the local name for the flowers. People would visit the Ford meadows from all over the county on Fraucup Sunday, the second Sunday in May, to admire and pick the flowers by the armful. Many of these made their way to the markets of Oxford and London. The fritillaries were first recorded in Ford in 1736, but local legend has it that they were escapees from the Tudor gardens at Waldridge Manor. The seeds were washed downstream on Ford Brook to the Ford meadows, where they established themselves. They later moved downstream to Thame, and then on to the meadows of Magdalen College in Oxford, which is still renowned for its spring display of the flowers.

Our ancient water meadows have been lost at a dramatic rate since the Second World War, with modern farming techniques leaving most of them dry and over-grazed. The fate of the snake's head fritillary highlights the plight of our natural wonders when they are not properly cared for and cherished. As drainage systems were installed around fields the damp conditions required by the fritillaries were lost, and the use of fertiliser raised nutrient levels, making the soil too rich for them. Ploughing and intensive grazing leave any surviving plants with little chance to grow, flower and shed their ripened seeds. A recent hunt around the village of Ford resulted in a mere two flowers found growing by the side of a road. Fraucup Meadow was dry, had been grazed to the ground and was bare of any wildflowers at all. While today it would be a thrill to find two of these rare flowers on such an unprotected and unmanaged site, thousands thrived there as recently as fifty years ago.

But thanks to the careful management and dedication of Berkshire, Buckinghamshire and Oxfordshire Wildlife Trust, we can at least continue to enjoy the spectacle of these lovely fritillaries flowering en masse in a traditional water meadow. They are one of our most precious floral treasures, and we should value and protect them for ever.

Sue Croxford, 2016

Tall Nettles

Tall nettles cover up, as they have done
These many springs, the rusty harrow, the plough
Long worn out, and the roller made of stone:
Only the elm butt tops the nettles now.

This corner of the farmyard I like most:
As well as any bloom upon a flower
I like the dust on the nettles, never lost
Except to prove the sweetness of a shower.

Edward Thomas, c. *1915*

Soon the plum blossom came out on the knotted black tree which climbed all over the Irishmen's Place, at the gable of one of the buildings, covering the long window slits with a network of close branches. A chaffinch built her nest in a crook in its boughs. Cream petals came thick among the pointed leaves of the pear trees, and a little brown bird lived right in the midst of the fragrance. Susan could put her head out of her mother's window and peep at the bright eyes among the leaves.

The double white lilac at the garden gate and the purple and lavender bushes hanging over the pig-cotes budded, and the lovely soft apple-green leaves burst through the javelin points. Starlings built in the hole in the giant apple tree which overshadowed the lawn and horse-trough, the ancient tree taller than Windystone itself, perhaps older, hollow as a skull, yet soon to be covered with blossom and little green fruit.

Doves cooed in the larch plantation, under the blue-speckled sky, jays screamed in the spinney and flashed their wings defiantly at the stealthy gamekeepers.

Magnificent pheasants rang out their challenge as they flew boldly clattering over the garden to the Druid Wood. Squirrels ran up and down the mossy walls and chased each other up the nut trees by the cow-sheds. A yellow stoat crept warily over the wall by the yew trees and rats slunk in the shadows of the stack-yard towards a hen-coop. The cock crew with a shrill note and the hen clucked to her chicks and cried fiercely, with flapping wings. The shadow of a hawk went over the young chickens, death in the blue sky, and every chick ran obediently to its mother, except one tiny stray upon which the savage claws and beak swooped.

Tom Garland ran out with his double-barrelled gun many a time a day, for it was Nature's birth time, and the little creatures were in danger from their enemies. The men had been busy since early in the year with the sheep, and now the lambs were merry curly-haired little rogues, with twinkling eyes and black sturdy legs.

They spent their baby days in Whitewell field, near the house, cropping a few morsels of short sweet grass, nuzzling and suckling from their mothers, and playing like school-children.

A lamb ran calling plaintively after a sheep, but she walked on, eating steadily, heartless, as he tried to push under her. He stood, puzzled, his first disillusion, and then, bleating and crying, he found his own true mother. With tail wagging and little firmly planted legs, he drank until the impatient mother gave him a push and sent him off to play. He stared round and then galloped to the others who were in the midst of a game.

Every year, for two hundred years at least, lambs ran the same race in Whitewell field. In other fields they had their odd games, but here it was always the same.

By the side of one of the paths stood the oak tree, with the seat under it, and a short distance away stood the great spreading ash. The lambs formed up in a line at the oak, and at some signal they raced to the ash, as fast as their tiny legs would go; then they wheeled round and tore back again. They held a little talk, a consultation, nose-rubbing, friendly pushes, and then off they went again on their race-track.

On the first of May the cows left their winter quarters in

the cow-houses, and were turned out to graze in the fields. That was a day to remember. Becky put her hands on her hips and shouted with laughter at their antics as they came pushing, tumbling through the gate and galloped wildly up and down the hills, with outstretching tails and tossing horns. They flung their heads back and blorted, they stamped their feet on the cool soft earth, they leapt like young lambs and danced with their unwieldy bodies on their slender legs.

Cows that had long been jealous attacked each other with curved horns, and the farmer and Dan stood ready with forks and sticks to prevent any harm. They raised their noses in the air and sniffed the smells of spring, and they ran to the streams and water-troughs, trampling the clear fresh water, drinking deeply with noisy gulps. They explored their old haunts, rubbed their flanks against their favourite stumps and railings, scratched their heads, polished their horns, and then settled down to eat the young short sweet grass.

The bull in the byre stamped and roared to be free with them, but he was dangerous, his horns were short and deep, and his eyes red. No man turned his back on him, but Tom never let him think he was master. They had had some tussles and he obeyed the farmer, but old Joshua kept away from him.

There were deaths as well as births on the farm, losses as well as gains. One day a man was seen waving and shouting as he came running across the Alder Lease. Tom stood at the back door, looking down the hill at the meadows below, straining to hear what he said. It was the servant from Oak Meadows and he pointed as he ran to a hollow by a wall out of sight. When he got near enough the words floated up the hill, 'A cow has fallen in the ditch yonder.'

'Get the ropes, quick,' cried Tom, with fear in his voice, and he and Dan ran down the fields with the heavy ropes and Joshua followed with a spade. Becky went too, to give a hand in pulling the poor beast, and Margaret stood pale and anxious at the door.

There it lay on its back where it had slipped in the wet treacherous grass, as it tried to get the bright patch across the little ditch. A child could have scrambled out, but the cow's legs were twisted, and it moaned very softly.

They put the ropes round it and hauled, but the sloping field and sudden drop made it difficult, the five of them could not move it. It lay with agonised eyes, imploring help. Its leg was broken, perhaps its back was injured, and above was the blue sky and larks singing.

'Get the gun and cartridge,' muttered Tom, and Becky hurried up the steep hills and across the fields. But it was too late, it was dead, and there it lay, a great white lump, smeared with mud and grass. They walked up the hill a sad procession, weary, disheartened. Margaret met them, troubled.

The next day a knacker took it away, some silver for the skin, that was all. It went down the hill with its legs sticking out, tragic and unreal, and an empty stall had to be filled.

Then someone, one of those folk who walk up and down the hills staring at nothing and asking foolish questions, left the gates open. Duchess's foal, a chestnut with a star, glossy as the nut itself, got out and ran in his young innocence to the new horse who was a kicker. He let fly, and Prince was lamed, and spoilt.

They had the vet, and his leg was rubbed and fomented, but he would always limp. Tom grew grave and worked harder than ever. Susan's heart burst with sorrow, but between herself and the grown-ups existed a barrier she could never cross.

Days grew longer and the mists of dawn were swept away by the sun growing stronger. Heavy scents of earth itself filled the air as the plough turned up the deep brown soil. Duchess and Diamond walked up and down the ploughland, and Dan guided them in the hollows and low hills as he drew the straight lines on the earth. Thrushes sang on the sycamore trees which stood round the walls of the ploughland, with long, pink, swelling buds.

Primroses made pale pools of light under the hedges, and along the steep banks, where they grew in spite of winds which suddenly swept up the valleys and over the hills with a fierceness which tore the blossom from the pear trees. But the flowers of the banks were small, short-stalked little ones, whilst those under last year's leaves in the hedgerows were large and fine.

Margaret, Becky, and Susan went off to the fields to pick cowslips, for the time had come to make cowslip wine. It was a cowslip day, too, a day of scents and pale gold colours, of glittering budded trees and little winds which clasped their skirts and tickled their ankles. The sky was fair, soft, yellow as a cowslip ball, and clouds like butterflies flew across it.

Alison Uttley, The Country Child, *1931*

Sonnet 98

From you have I been absent in the spring,
When proud-pied April dress'd in all his trim
Hath put a spirit of youth in every thing,
That heavy Saturn laugh'd and leap'd with him.
Yet nor the lays of birds nor the sweet smell
Of different flowers in odour and in hue
Could make me any summer's story tell,
Or from their proud lap pluck them where they grew;
Nor did I wonder at the lily's white,
Nor praise the deep vermilion in the rose;
They were but sweet, but figures of delight,
Drawn after you, you pattern of all those.
Yet seem'd it winter still, and, you away,
As with your shadow I with these did play.

William Shakespeare, published 1609

The bridge was bustling with traffic. Cars queued at the traffic lights as they made their way to the busy retail park. Underneath the bridge, a river cut through the concealed woodland, and the sound of rushing water drowned out the engine noises above. Hidden away from civilisation, the wooded area showed few signs of human interaction and this absence was clear in the abundance of birds fluttering about. Although quiet in the winter, with spring well on its way the woodland was thriving.

Further down the river where the water was calmer, both a male and female dipper could be seen along the water's edge. They worked hard to collect nest material for their first brood of the season. The adults searched for mosses and twigs, carrying them in their beaks up to the nest site in a concealed spot along the riverbank, a ledge in an old stone wall, of which they were just finishing the outer edges. Soon enough it was complete, and the female was perched inside incubating her eggs. Spreading her wings, she kept them warm, ensuring that the chicks inside would develop.

Once hatched, the young dippers were helpless in their initial days of life. It was time for the adults to start the relentless feeding, to give them the strength to survive once out of the nest. They worked together – both were on feeding duty, the male doing the main foraging while the female stayed in the nest, keeping the juveniles warm and safe. He would be in and out for the majority of each day, constantly slipping into the water to catch food. Arriving back, the adult would be greeted by each bird noisily asking to be fed, their beaks wide open, all fighting for the tasty food.

As the days passed, they grew and grew and the nest started to feel cramped. The juveniles were getting bigger every day and gaining their grey feathers.

Soon enough, it would be time. Time for them to take that huge step and leave the nest. Their wings were not strong enough to fly out like the adults would do many times a day, so this leap of faith really was the first challenge.

It took a few false starts before a juvenile left, dropping into the running water below and floating downstream a little before climbing onto a rock. Making its way towards the adult dippers, the juvenile was soon rewarded with some well-deserved food. Getting used to the running water and foraging was the second challenge.

The juvenile explored the sandbank, curiously dipping its head into the edges of the water. In one quick movement the world changed: the rushing water transformed into an eerie stillness, and the bright day into a blue-tinted world. Everything moved much more slowly in the water.

Or so it seemed.

The current pulled this way and that, and trying to catch those tiny insects hiding in the stony substrate proved harder than it originally seemed. Scrambling back to dry land, the juvenile realised that, for now, it was easier to make a lot of noise and wait for the adult to arrive with food.

With each day came more practice: stretching their wings and flying just that bit further each time; using their wings underwater to stabilise their weight and stay under; learning how to grip the unsettled substrate with their strong feet, staying below for a few extra seconds and grabbing the insects and fish.

After a couple of weeks the juveniles were becoming independent, no longer relying on the adults for food. Flying was second nature now, giving them freedom to go wherever they pleased. It was time to move on, fly away from home and find their own territory. Become adults.

Katie Halsall, 2016

Spring drew on: she was indeed already come; the frosts of winter had ceased; its snows were melted, its cutting winds ameliorated. My wretched feet, flayed and swollen to lameness by the sharp air of January, began to heal and subside under the gentler breathings of April; the nights and mornings no longer by their Canadian temperature froze the very blood in our veins; we could now endure the play-hour passed in the garden: sometimes on a sunny day it began even to be pleasant and genial, and a greenness grew over those brown beds, which, freshening daily, suggested the thought that Hope traversed them at night, and left each morning brighter traces of her steps. Flowers peeped out amongst the leaves; snow-drops, crocuses, purple auriculas, and golden-eyed pansies. On Thursday afternoons (half-holidays) we now took walks, and found still sweeter flowers opening by the wayside, under the hedges.

I discovered, too, that a great pleasure, an enjoyment which the horizon only bounded, lay all outside the high and spike-guarded walls of our garden: this pleasure consisted in prospect of noble summits girdling a great hill-hollow, rich in verdure and shadow; in a bright beck, full of dark stones and sparkling eddies. How different had this scene looked when I viewed it laid out beneath the iron sky of winter, stiffened in frost, shrouded with snow! – when mists as chill as death wandered to the impulse of east winds along those purple peaks, and rolled down 'ing' and holm till they blended with the frozen fog of the beck! That beck itself was then a torrent, turbid and curbless: it tore asunder the wood, and sent a raving sound through the air, often thickened with wild rain or whirling sleet; and for the forest on its banks, *that* showed only ranks of skeletons.

April advanced to May: a bright serene May it was; days of blue sky, placid sunshine, and soft western or southern gales filled up its duration. And now vegetation matured with vigour; Lowood shook loose its tresses; it became all green, all flowery; its great elm, ash, and oak skeletons were restored to majestic life; woodland plants sprang up profusely in its recesses; unnumbered varieties of moss filled its hollows, and it made a strange ground-sunshine out of the wealth of its wild primrose plants: I have seen their pale gold gleam in overshadowed spots like scatterings of the sweetest lustre.

Charlotte Brontë, Jane Eyre*, 1847*

Spring, and the children have the sort of infectious, giddy, butterfly restlessness they do on windy days. I can feel it too. Walking through the woods to school, there is so much to see: late frogspawn bobs below the surface of the pond like jelly with eyes and a comma butterfly basks on a tree stump, scallop-edged wings like pencil sharpenings. A few more children stop to see what we are looking at and the butterfly folds its wings as their shadows fall on it, pleating its bright colours into dark camouflage. I point out the little white punctuation mark on each wing that is newly familiar to some of the children, a comma that indicates the term the butterfly must serve in its life sentence: the torpor of hibernation. They like this, they think it's neat. This is one butterfly they will remember.

Then, in the woods behind school, in the low crook of a birch, a drift of downy fluff has collected into the shape of an owl. It is an owl: a tawny owlet, around twenty-five days old and very recently out of its nest. Covered in dove-grey, softly barred feathers, its round face has an aged, pinkish appearance. Against the white and damson ribbons of the peeling birch bark, it is well camouflaged.

It gazes at us, unblinking, with huge eyes. We keep our distance. The parents will be watching nearby, weighing their response to the unknown threat we pose. We show other children and parents, who are delighted but concerned – something must be wrong. I find myself doing some urgent PR. It's fine, I reassure them. Baby owls often plop out of trees, branching out from the nest hole before they can fly, or sometimes, balancing to poo off the edge of the nest, they fall out backwards (the children are beside themselves with the thought of this). They can climb back up. I even identify Mum for them, although we can't see her, showing the children how to listen for the mixed flock of little birds haranguing her further off.

Some of the children remind me of what happened the previous autumn. A neighbour brought me a dead tawny owl that had swooped in front of her car and been killed instantly and unavoidably. She was mortified, but thought I'd like to see it. I had better plans than that. Apart from a half-closed eye, it appeared undamaged. I took it into school. Any apprehension or squeamishness from the children disappeared as soon as they saw the owl, not quite believing it was real. They crowded round, incredulous, thrilled, and of course because the bird was dead there was no need to be quiet and they could touch it as much as they wanted. They felt the depth and density of the layered feathers, the sharpness of its beak, its great furred legs and curved claws and explored the strange-shaped, gripping Brillo pads on its feet. When I spread the wings out, like a dappled Spanish fan, they saw into a wood at night and gasped in awe. I pulled out my hand lens to show them the fringed feather edges that soften and lull wind resistance to an absolute hush. For a few moments then there was silence, and something like reverence; the bird was so alive for them that they seemed to be waiting for it to wake up and fly away. It lived in their imaginations for a long time.

We track the tawny owlet over the next two days and discover a sibling. Both are quite mobile, appearing in different trees at different heights among a natural trellis of ivy and honeysuckle vine. But there is still concern as to whether all is well. One has a lost, lopsided look. Shouldn't something be done? Surely the parents have abandoned them?

On the third afternoon, at ten past three, one of the chicks is leaning sleepily against the buttress of an oak like a remnant snowman, its head as big as its body. It has one eye half open and is just yards from the school gates. It is oddly conspicuous: a fine, graphite pencil drawing propped against a technicolour photographic background. I make a decision. It can't stay where it is and I am going to have to hide it.

I scout out a tree eight steps away, scanning for signs of the adults. I pull my thin coat over my hands, tie my hood tightly around my face and pick up the little bird. Too young to defend itself, there is no hissing or beak-snapping and its ineffectual wings remain folded like the pages of an old, foxed book. Its soft body is warm and I can feel the lightness of its hollow bones. I clasp the owlet to me and creep, head lowered in half-anticipation, to the safer place I have chosen.

I never heard her coming.

The element of surprise is exquisite. Her attack is succinct, well aimed and performed in absolute silence. The sudden whack on the side of my head is decisive and slightly muffled, like a blow from the sweeping end of a broom or a cricket ball hidden in a cushion, a *whumpf*, where the only sound comes from the bird's contact with me. I feel the passing rasp of a talon dulled by a layer of nylon.

I never even saw her.

I keep my head down and act quickly, placing the chick out of obvious sight, and retreat. Had I felt her presence and turned, my left eye would have been exposed and probably met her talon. I think of the pioneering wildlife photographer Eric Hosking, who famously lost his left eye to a tawny mother in 1939.

My attacker calls a series of soft, low '*kwicks*' to her chick in comfort and reassurance. It answers. We are all OK. I can hear the children coming out of school. I lower my hood and reach to feel a spot of blood, my left ear still ringing from the cuff. I can't stop grinning. It was a thrilling encounter. For a moment, I felt what it might be like to be a bank vole.

Nicola Chester, 2016

Spring

Nothing is so beautiful as Spring –
When weeds, in wheels, shoot long and lovely and lush;
Thrush's eggs look like little low heavens, and thrush
Through the echoing timber does so rinse and wring
The ear, it strikes like lightnings to hear him sing;
The glassy peartree leaves and looms, they brush
The descending blue; that blue is all in a rush
With richness; the racing lambs too have fair their fling.
What is all this juice and all this joy?
A strain of the earth's sweet being in the beginning
In Eden garden. – Have, get before it cloy,
Before it cloud, Christ lord, and sour with sinning,
Innocent mind and Mayday in girl and boy,
Most, O maid's child, thy choice and worth the winning.

Gerard Manley Hopkins, 1877

In the two months from the end of the third week of March to the end of the third week of May, there is accomplished the most rapid contrast of the year: a few summer birds may have come to us before this period begins, but with these few exceptions it includes the arrival of all our summer birds; the transition from cold to warmth; from dark bare branches to thick green trees. It is well sometimes to heighten the enjoyment of the best days of May by recalling some typical day of the preceding March. An instance may be taken from salmon-fishing in spring. The angler had spent a week on the river Spey in March, and one day in particular dwelt in his mind. As far as sport was concerned, it had not been unsuccessful, and when that is so, no stress of weather can destroy his pleasure. About three o'clock in the afternoon, bent on turning a day of fair into one of really good sport, he was advancing into a broad strong stream to wade as far out as the current would allow and as deep as he dared to go: a blizzard met him full in the face, with buffeting wind and blinding multitudes of snowflakes: the deciduous trees were stark and bare: in that stern week there was little song in the woods even of thrush or wren: on the river, apart from dippers, the only lively and constant evidence of birds was the presence of black-headed gulls and oyster-catchers. The latter birds are very noisy at that time of year. They are often in parties of three, and the exceeding restlessness gives the impression that two birds are perpetually trying to escape from the presence of a third, whose company is tedious and unwelcome; but whether this is an intrusive male or a superfluous female, I cannot say, for the sexes are alike in plumage, and I have not observed the birds to fight, as rival males would probably do.

Such were the conditions and the aspect of the place in March. In the latter part of May the angler was there once more; he had chanced on a cold week of March; it was now one of the warm weeks of May. The river was still broad and in fair order, though not so full as in March: the fishing had declined from good to fair: but it was sufficient to keep him keen and at work. There came a moment when the contrast with March was thought of and enjoyed. Again he was wading deep in the stream; behind him were some acres covered with whin, broom, wild raspberry and other wilful growths: in these thickets were some sedge-warblers and white-throats, and their songs came to him repeatedly; the sun shone warmly, the broom was coming out, but the whin was in full flower and fragrance; a light breeze brought the wonderful scent about him. Is the whole air ever so wonderfully and gratefully fragrant as when it is pervaded by the scent of whin? New-mown hay or a beanfield in flower are rare delights, but the flower of whin is best of all. The scent is fresh and invigorating, and yet so rich and luscious that it suggests apricots: it is as if the apricot had been designed in order to transmute part of the excellence of the scent of whin into something that could be perceived by another sense than that of smell. At any rate, both the scent and the fruit have this in common, that each is only to be known to perfection when warm in a hot sun. The whin is suited to the British climate; it needs no hot weather to enable it to flower and ripen its seeds. A cool summer does not discontent it; but it cannot endure extreme cold, and is grateful for our mild winters: it is essentially a plant for a gulf-stream climate. A stray flower of whin may be picked, so far as anything so prickly can be picked at all, on most bushes in every month of the year; but it is in May that every bush of whin is a glorious blaze of colour. Later in the summer, on a warm day there is a sporadic ticking noise amongst the whins: it is the opening of the dry seed-pods.

But I have now digressed enough. It is difficult when writing of outdoor things to keep to one subject, even that of birds – the world, as Robert Louis Stevenson says, 'is so full of a number of things' – and it is time to return to the proper subject of the book. The oyster-catchers are still about the river in May, but they are less noisy and restless than they were in March. They have eggs to attend to. These are laid out on shingle, with no attempt by the bird to hide them; but their pattern is so cunningly devised that the whole bed of shingle is their concealment.

To the bird life on the river, May has now added two common species of summer birds – terns and sandpipers. The flight of terns is graceful, light and airy, a delight to the eye; the voice is harsh. Sandpipers give an impression of happy affection, as a pair flit about together, piping pleasantly as if each enjoyed the other's company. My recollection is that both birds pipe; but there are details like this that one may for years take for granted, and then suddenly question with a desire for more particular observation.

To all this must be added the full song of woodland birds; the long vibrating notes of curlews, the first fresh green of deciduous trees and geans with their abundant delicate white flower. Year after year all this loveliness for eye and ear recurs: in early days, in youth, it was anticipated with confidence; in later years, as the season approaches, experience and age qualify the confidence with apprehension lest clouds of war or civil strife, or some emergency of work, or declining health, or some other form of human ill may destroy the pleasure or even the sight of it: and when once again it has been enjoyed we have a sense of gratitude greater than in the days of confident and thoughtless youth. Perhaps the memory of those days, having become part of our being, helps us in later life to enjoy each passing season. In every May, with the same beauty of sight and sound, 'we do beget that golden time again'.

Sir Edward Grey, The Charm of Birds, *1927*

May

May. 2. Tortoise marches about: eats part of a piece of cucumber-paring.

May. 6. Made a hot-bed for the hand glasses. I opened a hen swift, which a cat had caught, & found she was in high condition, very plump & fat: in her body were the rudiments of several eggs, two of which were larger than the rest, & would probably have been produced this season. Cats often catch swifts as they swoop to go up under the eaves of low houses. The cock red-breast is a gallant bird, & feeds his hen as they hop about on the walks, who receives his bounty with great pleasure, shivering with her wings, & expressing much complacency.

[Inserted leaf]
The quantity of rain that fell at Selborne between May 1st, 1779, & May 1st, 1780.

	inch	hund
In May, 1779	2	71
June	2	0
July	5	35
August	2	12
September	3	22
October	4	03

November	2	66
December	6	28
January, 1780	1	80
February	1	03
March	1	92
April	3	57
	36	69

May. 7. Wild cherries in bloom make a fine show in my hedges.

May. 8. The *Lathraea sqammaria* grows also on the banks of Trimming's orchard, just above the dry wall, opposite Grange-yard.

May. 10. Stormy all night. Tortoise scarce moves during this wet time. *Tremella nostoc* abounds on the grass walks.

May. 11. Tortoise moves about, but does not feed yet.

May. 12. The missel-thrush drives the mag-pies, & Jays from the garden. Lettuces that stood the winter come to use. Hops are poled, but make weak shoots.

May. 13. Vines are backward in their shoots, but show rudiments of fruit. The cores of the spruce-firs, produced last year, now fall. After a fast of 7 or 8 months, the tortoise which in Oct. 1779 weighed 6 pounds 9 oun: & ½ averdupoise, weights now only 6 pounds 4 ounces. Timothy began to break his fast May 17 on the globe-thistle, & American willow-herb; his favourite food is lettuce & dandelion, cucumber, & kidney-beans.

May. 16. Wheat looks somewhat yellow. Men sow barley: but the ground is cold, & cloddy.

May. 18. Field-crickets in their pupa-state lie-out before their holes. Magpies tear the missel-thrushes nest to pieces, & swallow the eggs.

May. 19. *Helleborus viridis* sheds its seeds in my garden, & produces many young plants.

May. 27. Large blue flag iris blows. Flesh-flies abound. Timothy the tortoise possesses a much greater share of discernment than I was aware of: & '. . . Is much too wise to go into a well;' for when he arrives at the haha, he distinguishes the fall of the ground, & retires with caution, or marches carefully along the edge: he delights in crawling up the flower-bank, & walking along its verge.

May. 29. The tortoise shunned the heat, it was so intense.

May. 30. Columbines, a fine variegated sort, blow.

May. 31. Master Etty went on board the Vansittart India-man at Spithead. Thunderstorm in the night with a fine shower.

Reverend Gilbert White, The Naturalist's Journal, *1780*

Ah, May is bounding forward! Her silly heart leaps at the sight of the old place – and so in good truth does mine. What a pretty place it was – or rather, how pretty I thought it! I suppose I should have thought any place so where I had spent eighteen happy years. But it was really pretty. A large, heavy, white house, in the simplest style, surrounded by fine oaks and elms, and tall massy plantations shaded down into a beautiful lawn, by wild overgrown shrubs, bowery acacias, ragged sweet-briars, promontories of dogwood, and Portugal laurel, and bays overhung by laburnum and bird-cherry; a long piece of water letting light into the picture, and looking just like a natural stream, the banks as rude and wild as the shrubbery, interspersed with broom, and furze, and bramble, and pollard oaks covered with ivy and honeysuckle; the whole enclosed by an old mossy park paling, and terminating in a series of rich meadows, richly planted. This is an exact description of the home which, three years ago, it nearly broke my heart to leave. What a tearing up by the root it was! I have pitied cabbage-plants and celery, and all transplantable things, ever since; though, in common with them, and with other vegetables, the first agony of the transportation being over, I have taken such firm and tenacious hold of my new soil, that I would not for the world be pulled up again, even to be restored to the old beloved ground; – not even if its beauty were undiminished, which is by no means the case; for in those three years it has thrice changed masters, and every successive possessor has brought the curse of improvement upon the place; so that between filling up the water to cure dampness, cutting down trees to let in prospects, planting to keep them out, shutting up windows to darken the inside of the house (by which means one end looks precisely as an eight of spades would do that should have the misfortune to lose one of his corner pips), and building colonnades to lighten the out, added to a general clearance of pollards, and brambles, and ivy, and honeysuckles, and park palings, and irregular shrubs, the poor place is so transmogrified, that if it had its old looking-glass, the water, back again, it would not know its own face. And yet I love to haunt round about it: so does May. Her particular attraction is a certain broken bank full of rabbit burrows, into which she insinuates her long pliant head and neck, and tears her pretty feet by vain scratchings: mine is a warm sunny hedgerow, in the same remote field, famous for early flowers. Never was a spot more variously flowery: primroses yellow, lilac white, violets of either hue, cowslips, oxslips, arums, orchises, wild hyacinths, ground ivy, pansies, strawberries, heart's-ease, formed a small part of the Flora of that wild hedgerow. How profusely they covered the sunny open slope under the weeping birch, 'the lady of the woods' – and how often have I started to see the early innocent brown snake, who loved the spot as well as I did, winding along the young blossoms, or rustling amongst the fallen leaves! There are primrose leaves already, and short green buds, but no flowers; not even in that furze cradle so full of roots, where they used to blow as in a basket. No, my May, no rabbits! no primroses! We may as well get over the gate into the woody winding lane, which will bring us home again.

Here we are making the best of our way between the old

elms that arch so solemnly over head, dark and sheltered even now. They say that a spirit haunts this deep pool – a white lady without a head. I cannot say that I have seen her, often as I have paced this lane at deep midnight, to hear the nightingales, and look at the glow-worms; – but there, better and rarer than a thousand ghosts, dearer even than nightingales or glow-worms, there is a primrose, the first of the year; a tuft of primroses, springing in yonder sheltered nook, from the mossy roots of an old willow, and living again in the clear bright pool. Oh, how beautiful they are – three fully blown, and two bursting buds! How glad I am I came this way! They are not to be reached. Even Jack Rapley's love of the difficult and the unattainable would fail him here: May herself could not stand on that steep bank. So much the better. Who would wish to disturb them? There they live in their innocent and fragrant beauty, sheltered from the storms, and rejoicing in the sunshine, and looking as if they could feel their happiness. Who would disturb them? Oh, how glad I am I came this way home!

Mary Russell Mitford, 'The First Primrose', Our Village, *1824*

My children called it Dad's field. It was a place where they could wander through the long grass, hurtle down the hill, chase butterflies or simply enjoy the sense of freedom that being outside gives a child. Despite its official title within the family, it never was my field; it belonged to the Lancashire Wildlife Trust, as it still does. I simply looked after it as a voluntary warden, a relaxing task that enabled me to get to know the site intimately. I knew the location of the adder's tongue and where to find the globeflower, I knew the flush that emerged halfway up the slope on the east side that gave rise to the marsh valerian and the greater bird's foot trefoil. I knew the areas of vegetation that held the most species and those that had the least.

It is a site unknown to the general public and probably little known even to the keen naturalist. No casual traveller would see it, unless they were seated in one of the railway carriages that regularly flashed by along the line that marked its western boundary. A hedge and another field delineated the north side, a small brook lay to the south, while the eastern edge merged into the woodland that extended further down the valley. Sit on the slope and look east and south Lancashire unfolds before you, the brook disappearing into the Yarrow woods which in turn spill over the base of the valley, which has as its backdrop the grey-blue of the Pennine hills.

In many ways the field was not particularly remarkable. It held no exceptionally rare species, it had no complex mix of habitats and no unique geological features. What was remarkable, however, was its survival. Species-rich grassland, either as meadow or pasture, was once common across Britain, the product of centuries of farming with scythe, cattle or sheep which was attuned to address local needs. But sadly, since the end of the Second World War these low-input grasslands and the attitudes that went with them have been replaced by uniform fields hosting rye grass, clover and very little else. Indeed, by the time the significance of these once-common habitats had been realised and their conservation called for, it was almost too late. Lowland Lancashire had only two such sites remaining; Dad's field was one of them.

On greyer, more reflective solo days at the reserve, the realisation of what had been lost countrywide induced a gentle melancholy. However such sadness was virtually impossible when visiting in spring sunshine. The wealth of colour, the variation in leaf pattern, the ever-changing vegetation and the discoveries that came from exploring it gave an innate sense of quiet joy. It was partly this joy and partly the distinctiveness of the vegetation that led me to visit the site for another reason every spring – this time in my role as lecturer in botany, tasked with the specific job of developing undergraduate identification skills and, more generally, an appreciation of plants. I ran the course every spring, visiting a mixture of inspirational sites over two weeks to develop the students' breadth of knowledge. From an academic viewpoint the slope provided an excellent example of an MG5c *Cynosurus cristatus-Centaurea nigra* grassland, *Danthonia decumbens* sub-community. From a wider perspective the magic of the place, its diversity, its glimpse into the past and its view over the countryside provided a stimulus that helped win students over to the joys of plants.

It was the academic viewpoint that was of initial priority one day every year in late May as the students entered the site by the gate, split into small groups and then set out their tape measures to delineate their survey areas. They then adopted the standard botanical survey position of 'head down and bottom up' as they got into the intricacies of the meadow. A colleague and I would move between groups addressing general queries, drawing attention to species missed and discussing the finer points of identification. Once finished we would turn our faces back to the wider landscape and enjoy a picnic.

A scientific approach emphasises increasing breadth of knowledge and a resultant search for universalities. Our field visit aimed to give wider understanding of grasslands generally. From a teaching point of view the site was an infallible source of species that typified a meadow community. Ostensibly nothing changed and students invariably identified the same community each year. However, intimacy with the site made me realise that it never actually was the same year on year. Some changes were obvious: the extinction of globeflower, the arrival of speckled woods, the thick thatch that supported a multitude of spiders revelling in the three-dimensional vegetation complexity that followed the removal of grazing in the year of Foot and Mouth. An eye seasoned by experience was needed to spot other changes: the abundance of spring sedge one year, the gradual increase of cuckoo flower and the variable difficulty of picking up the later-emerging grasses such as quaking grass and heath grass.

After almost twenty years, the appeal of the site hasn't lessened. I still take students there, I still teach them of the intricacies of an MG5. Equally important, I sometimes encourage them to change their focus and recognise that nature is a pleasure in itself. Within education it is currently fashionable to attempt to assess whether an activity has been successful. Of the twenty generations of students that surveyed the site, some are professional ecologists of various forms and many others have gone on to be employed in environmental roles. So technically the trip can be viewed as a success. More difficult to assess, however, is whether those former embryonic surveyors still find a place for nature in their lives. I suspect and hope that they do and I like to think that our spring experiences on a small Lancashire Wildlife Trust grassland reserve helped form their lives. The sense that this experience somehow shapes a person's future pleasures imbues my renewed acquaintance of the site each year with a sense of promise and reawakens my own connection to the place. Next spring I will take my granddaughters to a site their mother knew as a girl. I secretly hope they name it Grandad's field.

Paul Ashton, 2016

The Trees

The trees are coming into leaf
Like something almost being said;
The recent buds relax and spread,
Their greenness is a kind of grief.

Is it that they are born again
And we grow old? No, they die too.
Their yearly trick of looking new
Is written down in rings of grain.

Yet still the unresting castles thresh
In fullgrown thickness every May.
Last year is dead, they seem to say,
Begin afresh, afresh, afresh.

Philip Larkin, 1967

Imagine you're walking along a path that leads away from a vast and swaying reedbed, an hour or so before sunset. This is a landscape shaped by man: it may seem wild, but this part of the Suffolk coast is carefully managed for people and wildlife. As a stark reminder of our continual human impact, a nuclear power station broods in the background in harsh juxtaposition with the gentle landscape, its boxy shape and white dome contrasting with the natural curves and undulations of the coast, the cliffs and these famous nature reserves.

This is the season when the stage is set for the coming year: sorting the genetic lines that will survive, reproduce and prosper, from those that will fall by the wayside. Hobbies are snapping dragonflies off the surface of the water, while marsh harriers sweep the tops of the reedbed, passing food to their mates in a spectacular aerial display. Swifts and sand martins wheel against the darkening sky, and all around, the woods are alive with the rustling of unseen birds: chaffinches, robins, wrens, blue tits, blackbirds, blackcaps, whitethroats layered with the frenetic outbursts of Cetti's, sedge and reed warblers in the reeds. Underpinning them all on the bass, the booming of the bittern reverberates in the air and sends deep vibrations into the stomach of everyone that hears. Crows and jackdaws caw their harsh, uncouth tones and the yaffling of the green woodpecker adds a comical twist.

The sun is sinking over the reeds.

The final visitors, families and couples are strolling back to their cars along the high grassy bank that separates the sea from the marshes below. They are bathed in the golden light coming from the west. To the east, waves crash onto the shingle beach and terns dive for tiny, silver fish. Gulls (mostly black-headed) are crying harshly to one another, while on the marsh, avocets '*kluut-kluut*'. They may be beautiful birds with their strikingly elegant black and white plumage, but in reality they're bullies: pity any wader who strays too close, to be quickly and viciously driven off. The reeling of a grasshopper warbler, sounding uncannily like the whirring of a fishing line being fast let out, starts up: he can't be seen, but you can imagine his little head turning slowly and smoothly side to side to make sure that everyone can hear.

The sun is sinking over the marsh.

A little way down the road, the same woodland and grassland birds are in mid-song; only the reedbed and marshland dwellers are no longer heard. Instead, as the shadows lengthen, the forlorn and lonely cuckoo repeats his plaintive, yet hauntingly beautiful name, sending shivers up your spine and setting goosebumps at the back of your neck. He is calling out, but no one is answering him – not yet, anyway. He's the first back, but in a few weeks both rivals and lovers will return to take their place in the mating season.

The sun is sinking over the heathland.

The dulcet tones of the cuckoo are interrupted by a swift and throaty cackle from the nearby gorse. This new sound comes at first in fits and starts, as though warming up for a long and complex performance; then, as the calls of the warblers and tits and finches begin to lessen and grow faint, the nightingale takes up his place and shatters the stillness of the evening with his continuous crescendo of warbling, chirruping, rasping, snapping, whistling, squealing, clucking and clicking. He's a great pretender, taking pride in the unpredictability of his voice, challenging and imitating his adversaries, relentless and untiring. The most you'll see is a silhouette, a shadow, an outline; he lives to be admired for his song alone.

The sun is sinking over the gorse.

From over near the plantation comes a deeper, more nasal call, the unmistakable grunt of a roving woodcock as he circles above the treetops, wings beating frenetically. This complements the rough bark from a dog fox, and contrasts with the gentle mewling of one – no two – little owls in amicable conversation. Then, at first unrecognisable as it's so rarely heard, the high-pitched tones of the wailing stone curlew: a banshee. Still the nightingale continues his serenade, barely pausing, whilst the echoes of the cuckoo remain, and then, to add one last dimension, the purring of the now rare and elusive turtle dove briefly caresses the air, before falling silent.

The sun is sinking over the woodlands.

I don't think any artist, using the subtlest brush strokes and softest of hues, could capture the rich colours and sounds and scents of the evening. Is there a poet who could fit the rhythms and beats and randomness to the rigidity of a sonnet or haiku, even with the cleverest metaphors? No orchestra could mimic the mellow simplicity and the startling complexity of this unrehearsed, yet harmonised soundtrack.

The sun has set on this Suffolk spring evening.

Lucy McRobert, 2016

Author Biographies

Paul Ashton is currently head of Biology at Edge Hill University. A native of Lancashire, previous study and employment saw him happily exiled to Scotland and Norfolk before returning to the North West. For over twenty years he has striven to fire an enthusiasm for plants, evolution and conservation in his students. A mission he is still energetically engaged in.

Jane Austen (d. 1817) was a leading author of her time, writing several works of romantic fiction, including *Sense and Sensibility* (1811), *Pride and Prejudice* (1813), *Mansfield Park* (1814) and *Emma* (1815), which continue to be widely read today.

H. E. Bates' (d. 1974) works include *The Darling Buds of May* and *Fair Stood the Wind for France*. The countryside of Northamptonshire provided a great deal of inspiration for his writing, his love of nature clearly expressed in a wide variety of essays and short stories.

Ginny Battson is a professional nature and landscape photographer with a lifelong love of wildlife, especially that of woodlands and watery habitats. Her passions include environmental ethics, ecoliteracy and being a mother. She enjoys walking, wading, observing and writing her blog seasonalight.wordpress.com. She has lived in the US and New Zealand before returning to live in Wales.

R. D. Blackmore (d. 1900) was celebrated for his vibrant depictions of the English countryside in his works, particularly the area around Exmoor in Devon, which is portrayed in his most famous work, *Lorna Doone* (1869).

Charlotte Brontë (d. 1855) was the eldest of the three Brontë sisters, all novelists. Charlotte originally published her work under the pseudonym Currer Bell to disguise her gender. She wrote several novels, although her first, *Jane Eyre* (1847), has remained her best-known work.

Robert Browning (d. 1889) was one of the leading Victorian poets, famous for his dramatic monologues, and married to Elizabeth Barrett, also a respected poet. His most popular works include 'Childe Roland to the Dark Tower Came' (1855), 'Home-Thoughts, from Abroad' (1845) and 'The Pied Piper of Hamelin' (1842).

Jo Cartmell is a lifelong naturalist with a special interest in water voles and wild-flower meadows. She runs the Twitter accounts @WaterVole and @NearbyWild and also blogs for nearbywild.org.uk about her local wildlife.

Geoffrey Chaucer (d. 1400) was a poet in the Middle Ages, best known for *The Canterbury Tales*, a collection of stories written in the 1380s. Told from the point of view of a group of pilgrims travelling together from London to Canterbury, the tales provide an insight to English society at the time.

Nicola Chester writes about the wildlife she finds wherever she is, mostly roaming the North Wessex Downs where she lives with her husband and three children. She has written professionally for over a decade. Nicola is particularly passionate about engaging people with nature and how language can communicate the thrill of wild experiences. You can read her blog here: nicolachester.wordpress.com.

Ryan Clark is a 22-year-old professional ecologist based in Buckinghamshire. A lifelong wildlife recorder, he enjoys going for walks in the Chilterns, recording and photographing wildlife. His main passions are plants and pollinators, especially solitary bees. He loves sharing his passion for British wildlife with others and regularly blogs at ryanclarkecology.wordpress.com.

Will Cohu has written for many newspapers and magazines, and was a regular columnist for the *Daily Telegraph*. His books include *Urban Dog* (2001), *Out Of The Woods* (2007), *The Wolf Pit* (2012) and *Nothing But Grass* (2015). He has been twice shortlisted for the *Sunday Times* EFG Short Story Award and was shortlisted in 2013 for the PEN/Ackerley Prize for *The Wolf Pit*.

James Common is a dedicated naturalist, birder, writer and graduate conservation scientist from Northumberland. He is passionate about all aspects of natural history though his greatest interests lie in the realms of biological recording, ecology and ornithology. Elsewhere James is a keen blogger (commonbynature.co.uk) and a member of A Focus on Nature, the youth nature network.

Peter Cooper is a lifelong naturalist, completing his final year of zoology at the University of Exeter Penryn Campus at time of print. He specialises in the study and conservation of British mammals, as well as engaging others in nature through his blog (petecooperwildlife.wordpress.com), and as a committee member for Britain's youth nature network, A Focus on Nature.

Rob Cowen is an award-winning writer who has authored columns on nature for the *Independent* and the *Telegraph*. Described by the *Guardian* as 'one of the UK's most exciting nature writers', he received the Roger Deakin Award for his first book, *Skimming Stones*, in 2012. His latest book, *Common Ground*, was shortlisted for the Portico Prize 2015, and was selected as a 'Book Of The Year' in *The Times*.

Alan Creedon writes about the connections between people and the landscape, identity and the environment, and about himself as part of nature. From rural to urban, the need for nature connection runs deep in his work. He writes from a place of feeling and reflection to convey a situation or idea as experienced and as a process of discovery and learning.

Sue Croxford is a member of the Berkshire, Buckinghamshire and Oxfordshire Wildlife Trust and author of the Bug Mad Girl wildlife blog. The blog, which has been awarded *BBC Wildlife Magazine*'s blog of the week, can be found at www.bugmadgirl.blogspot.co.uk. Sue has also written magazine articles that have been published in *Best of British, Yours, Chiltern* and *Lymphoma Matters*.

Miriam Darlington writes a monthly column in the *Saturday Times*: the renowned Nature Notebook. Her previous books include *Windfall* (poetry) and *Otter Country* (a nature memoir about wild otters). She is currently working on a book about owls and humans. She teaches creative writing at Plymouth University, and lives in Devon.

Elliot Dowding is 22 years old and lives in Sussex, where he was born and raised. He has been passionate about wildlife since early childhood, thanks largely to encouragement from his parents. He is also a keen birder, though his interests vary from archaeology to book collecting. Elliot is currently pursuing his dream of a career in writing.

Thomas Furly Forster (d. 1825) was a botanist who compiled many lists and drawings of plants. After his death, his natural history journals were collated and published by his son as *The Pocket Encyclopaedia of Natural Phenomena*.

Chris Foster is a birdwatcher, gradually evolving into an all-round naturalist, based in Reading, Berkshire. On top of teaching associate and PhD positions at Reading University, Chris is an aspiring nature writer supported by A Focus On Nature, the youth conservation network. His wildlife blog is entering its sixth year; his work has also appeared in *Biosphere* and *Antenna* magazines.

Alexi Francis is an artist and illustrator living in Sussex. All her life she has been a lover of wildlife and studied zoology at university. She is interested in writing, especially about the natural world, and has had several articles published in anthologies and magazines such as *Earthlines*.

Kenneth Grahame (d. 1932) became renowned for his children's book *The Wind in the Willows*, based upon the bedtime stories of woodland creatures he told to his young son Alastair. He wrote numerous other stories and articles, but none were as well received as his great success, which continues to be popular today.

Caroline Greville is writing a book on her involvement with badgers in the context of her family life and wider rural setting. This memoir forms the main part of her PhD at the University of Kent, alongside research into new nature writing. She is Secretary of the East Kent Badger Group and teaches creative writing.

Sir Edward Grey (d. 1933) was a Liberal statesman, and the longest serving foreign secretary of the twentieth century (1905–16). He was also a keen ornithologist, and published *The Charm of Birds* in 1927, a record of his observations of birds and their song.

Katie Halsall is inspired by documenting life and raising awareness. With an interest in both wildlife conservation and photography, pursuing Wildlife Media BA (Hons) was the obvious next step after completing photography at college. In the past five years Katie has gained experience in photographic, film and written forms of media whilst studying and maintaining both personal and media blogs.

Thomas Hardy (d. 1928) wrote several famous works including *Far from the Madding Crowd* (1874), *The Mayor of Casterbridge* (1886) and *Tess of the d'Urbervilles* (1891). Rural society was a major theme in his books; most were set in the partly imagined region of Wessex, based largely on areas of south and southwest England.

Melissa Harrison's first novel, *Clay*, was about urban wildlife – among other things. Set in a rural village, her second, *At Hawthorn Time*, was shortlisted for the Costa Novel of the Year Award. She writes the Nature Notebook in *The Times*, and has a short book about rain due out from Faber and The National Trust in 2016.

Felicia Hemans' (d. 1835) first collection of poetry was published when she was just 14 years old. She went on to become a well-known literary figure; her most important works include *The Forest Sanctuary* (1825), *Records of Woman* and *Songs of the Affections* (1830).

Gerard Manley Hopkins (d. 1899) was a poet with a passion for writing descriptions of the natural world, with works including 'The Windhover' and 'The Sea and the Skylark'. He was also a priest and found himself conflicted between his religious belief and his poetry, giving the latter up for seven years at one point. Most of his poetry was not published during his lifetime.

A. E. Housman (d. 1936) was a classicist and poet, best known for *A Shropshire Lad*, a collection of sixty-three poems, including II ('Loveliest of Trees, the Cherry Now') and XXIX ('The Lent Lily').

Alice Hunter is a wildlife and landscape photographer with a particular interest in European flora and butterflies and a passion for sharing her love of the natural world through her work. She loves being outdoors and writes regularly for several branches of The Wildlife Trusts as well as blogging about her experiences. Visit www.hunterphotos.co.uk to see Alice's work.

Richard Jefferies (d. 1887) was a nature writer of both essays and novels, inspired by his upbringing on a farm. His works include *The Amateur Poacher* (1879), *Round About a Great Estate* (1880), *Nature Near London* (1883) and *The Life of the Fields* (1884). The collection *Field and Hedgerow* was published posthumously in 1889.

Samshad Khan is a poet and coach in creative writing, resilience and inspired living. She works with individuals, theatres and community groups. She uses writing as a tool to empower individuals and develop communities. Her poetry collection *Megalomaniac* is published by Salt Publishing. Shamshad is currently working on a show with the Horse and Bamboo puppet theatre. She blogs at: shamshadkhan27.wordpress.com

Reverend Francis Kilvert (d. 1879) was a clergyman who kept diaries recording his observations on rural life. His writings were collected, edited and published posthumously in three volumes from 1938 to 1940.

Philip Larkin (d. 1985) was a poet and novelist, best known for his poetry collections including *The Less Deceived* (1955), *The Whitsun Weddings* (1964) and *High Windows* (1974). He was the recipient of many honours, including the Queen's Gold Medal for Poetry in 1965.

D. H. Lawrence (d. 1930) wrote the famously explicit *Lady Chatterley's Lover* (1928), which led to an obscenity trial when published in its entirety in 1960. He also wrote almost 800 poems, of which the best known are based on themes of nature, including the collection *Birds, Beasts and Flowers* (1932).

Claire Leighton (d. 1989) was an artist, writer and illustrator famous for her work depicting scenes of rural life. Her best-known works include *The Farmer's Year: A Calendar of English Husbandry* (1933) and *Four Hedges: A Gardener's Chronicle* (1935).

Sir John Lister-Kaye is a naturalist, conservationist and author. He is the director of Aigas Field Centre, a nature centre in Scotland and the author of several books including *Song of the Rolling Earth: A Highland Odyssey* (2003), which established him as one of the UK's most respected nature writers.

Kate Long is the author of eight novels, including the *Sunday Times* number one bestseller *The Bad Mother's Handbook.* Her domestic comedy-drama has been adapted for radio and television and she has written for a range of newspapers and magazines such as *Good Housekeeping,* the *Telegraph* and *BBC Wildlife Magazine.* She is an enthusiastic ecologist and lives in Shropshire with her husband and two sons. www.katelongbooks.com

Lucy McRobert is the Nature Matters campaigns manager for The Wildlife Trusts. She has written for publications including *BBC Wildlife,* is a columnist for *Birdwatch* magazine and was the Researcher on Tony Juniper's *What Nature does for Britain* (2015). She is the creative director of A Focus On Nature, the youth nature network, and is a keen birdwatcher and mammal-watcher.

Vijay Medtia is a novelist and a short story writer based in Manchester. His regular trips to India have inspired his fiction, as have some of the great writers from the past. He likes John Steinbeck's quote, 'The writing profession makes horse racing seem like a solid stable business.' www.vijaymedtia.com

Mary Russell Mitford (d. 1855) wrote a series of stories that portrayed a fascinating picture of life in a rural community, based on her own village. Originally published in the *Lady's Magazine,* they were collected in to book form in 1824 as *Our Village,* her most famous work.

Stephen Moss is a naturalist, author and TV producer based on the Somerset Levels. He is president of the Somerset Wildlife Trust.

David North has been interested in wildlife and wild places as long as he can remember and his career includes working for National Trust, RSPB and for the last ten years at Norfolk Wildlife Trust. He lives in North Norfolk with his wife Tasha and at weekends can be found exploring the local coast between Cley Marshes and Salthouse.

George Orwell (d. 1950) was the pseudonym of Eric Arthur Blair, writer and critic best-known for his novels *Animal Farm* (1945) and *Nineteen Eighty-Four* (1949). He had a fondness for the natural world, often observing the changing of the seasons in his personal diaries.

Eleanor Parker is a historian and writer, with a doctorate in medieval English literature from the University of Oxford. Her research focuses on historical narratives in literature produced in England between *c.*1000 and *c.*1400. **'The Seafarer'** is an Old English poem from the point of view of a man alone at sea, recorded in the tenth century *Exeter Book*, a collection of Anglo-Saxon poetry.

William Shakespeare (d. 1616) was one of the world's greatest writers. He wrote about 154 sonnets and 38 plays, including *Romeo and Juliet, Hamlet* and *Macbeth,* which continue to be studied, performed and adapted all over the world to this day. His sonnets were published in 1609 but are believed to have been composed earlier.

Jo Sinclair was born in Cambridge and lives in rural south Cambridgeshire. She is a freelance writer and writes about local British natural history.

Melissa Spiers is a volunteer at Gloucestershire Wildlife Trust and former trainee of Dorset Wildlife Trust. During her traineeship Melissa was based on Chesil beach, and her experience of this dramatic place inspired her to write the piece in this book. Melissa is a keen amateur birder and wildlife lover in general. She hopes to work in conservation communication.

Edward Step (d. 1931) was the author of numerous books on nature, both popular and specialist, including *Favourite Flowers of the Garden and Greenhouse* (1896), *The Romance of Wild Flowers* (1901), *Nature in the Garden* (1910) and *Nature Rambles: An Introduction to Country-lore* (1930).

Adelle Stripe is the author of three collections of poetry including the award-winning *Dark Corners of the Land.* Based in West Riding she lectures at Manchester Writing School and is currently writing her debut novel, *Black Teeth,* based on the life and work of the Bradford playwright Andrea Dunbar. www.adellestripe.com

Peter Tate has published several books on ornithology, including *A Century of Bird Books* (1979), *Bird, Men and Books: A Literary History of Ornithology* (1986) and most recently *Flights of Fancy: Birds in Myth, Legend and Superstition* (2009).

Dylan Thomas (d. 1953) was a Welsh poet and writer. Although most famous for his poetry, including 'Do Not Go Gentle into That Good Night', his 'play for voices' *Under Milk Wood* is among his best-known works, having been adapted both for the stage and film.

Edward Thomas' (d. 1917) works were often noted for his portrayals of the English countryside, including *In Pursuit of Spring* (1914), *The Heart of England* (1906) and *The South Country* (1909).

Alison Uttley (d. 1976) frequently focused her writing on rural topics, including her 'Little Grey Rabbit' series of young children's tales and *The Country Child* (1931), based on her childhood experiences growing up on a farm.

Reverend Gilbert White (d. 1793) was a curate, as well as a keen naturalist and ornithologist. His best known work is *The Natural History and Antiquities of Selborne* (1789); his journals were published posthumously, in 1931. He is considered by many to have been a major influence in forming modern attitudes to and respect for nature.

Dorothy Wordsworth (d. 1855) kept diaries and wrote poetry, but *The Grasmere Journals* was not published until long after her death, in 1897. It contains an extract that was a source for her brother William Wordsworth's famous poem 'Daffodils'.

Annie Worsley is a mother of four and grandmother living on a coastal croft in the remote Northwest Highlands of Scotland. A former academic who explored the relationships between humans and environments in diverse parts of the world, including Papua New Guinea, she now writes about nature, wildlife and landscape. She tries to paint the wild using words.

COMING SOON IN THIS SERIES

The Seasons books aim to capture the changing year through evocative pieces of writing about nature, describing the life-cycles of flora and fauna, startling moments of transition, seasonal change in cities and gardens, wildlife experiences that epitomise a point in the year or the shifting patterns of country life.

Each book includes a collection of writing, old and new – extracts from classic texts, lesser-known historical material, new works from established nature writers and some pieces by Wildlife Trusts supporters throughout the UK – threaded together to mirror the unfolding of the seasons.

***Summer* – May 2016**

978-1-78396-244-0

***Autumn* – August 2016**

978-1-78396-248-8

***Winter* – November 2016**

978-1-78396-252-5